Still Life With Brass Pole

Craig Machen

Mark,

Thanks for having a look!

NOTE: I'm not sure if the blinking lights were in my trunk. I'm about 95% on that. We might have put them in my friend's car and then the law found me through him. There are also places where the passing of time forced me to recreate dialogue. What else? Oh yes, there are spots where I combined closely related events to keep the narrative moving. I also changed names – almost all of them. That, and I love dogs, and wish very much that I had been a Beatle (or at least a better guitar player).

To Zach and Sean,
my reasons for getting up in the morning, even before you
were born.

PART ONE

FLORIDA, OKLAHOMA, ARIZONA & TEXAS

(With a Few Hours in Kansas & New Mexico)

1

TARZAN BOY

Dean is driving the Porsche. In the passenger seat, I am drunk, coked to the gills, stoned and completely at ease. The car belongs to my dad, and so does Dean, figuratively speaking. He is Dad's lover. Of course, I'm not supposed to know this, so I am having to listen to Dean's smoke screen of make-believe female conquests. And in a bizarre way, Dean's performance, sort of like Jim Jay Bullock doing a Don Johnson impersonation, is making it all that much more fun.

We are in South Florida, somewhere outside of Pompano, in the tall pines. It is dark, the moon is full, and I am sixteen years old and on my way to the nudie bar. When I get back to Oklahoma I will tell no one. My friends won't believe me, my mother... well, who knows? And Andie, my girlfriend, would definitely break up, which would never do because she is the only person keeping tabs on me in a day to day way.

But here I am, hauling ass through the trees in an imported sports car in the age of *Miami Vice*. The tape deck is blaring; and given our destination, I wish it was *Highway To Hell* or *Everybody Wants Some*, but this is Dad's cassette collection so *Tarzan Boy* will have to do.

Dad is not here, but we have a few hundred of his dollars and his blessing. More than his blessing, we have his directive. Which means even Andie can't be mad. I've been sent by my father on a supervised errand - sort of – accompanied by a parent-ish figure. So I have to go. Right? It would be inhospitable not to.

Oh, Andie, please don't be mad. It just kind of happened (even as it happens). An hour ago Dad and I were hanging out in his bedroom. No big deal. Just chatting. Then the coke came out - I may have outright asked for it this time. And as he started to chop up the lines on an aluminum foil square on a TV tray, the conversation turned from, "Oh, you know how your mother is..." - I definitely do – to, "Cocaine was legal at the turn of the century. It's really not such a big deal... Sigmund Freud, Edgar Allen Poe, Sherlock Holmes, etc. etc."

"Oh sure," I responded in total, enthusiastic agreement, "Coca-Cola gets its name, blah, blah, blah..."

We were talking, talking, talking and he said, "Would you like to go to the strip club?"

And I, thinking, "Hell yes, I'd like to go to the strip club!" answered, "Sure," as though it weren't the pivotal moment of my young life.

But who cares how I got here, Andie. I am here, and you are a million miles away. Tonight I have a date with destiny at a gentlemen's cabaret. And isn't "cabaret" a silly euphemism. As if anything gentlemanly or artistic ever went on inside a "gentlemen's club" or a "cabaret."

Argghhh... You deserve a far better boyfriend than me. I'm not sure what you do when we're not together, but I'll bet it's never worse than PG. And look at me, rated X for adult situations, profanity, drug use and impending nudity. God I love nudity! But I love you so much more, and I'd do anything to be the responsible young man you so totally deserve. However, we both know that I am exactly the kind of boy who succumbs to this brand of temptation; and anyway, we are nearly there.

***

The coke thing started a couple of nights ago at my little sister's fourteenth birthday party. We were on a yacht owned by one of Dad's clients – the vice-president of some South American country - cruising the Intercoastal Waterway. The celebration was divided pretty evenly between Mary's friends, a lot of upper-middle class fourteen and fifteen year-olds, and Dad's business partners and employees. On one side of the boat the kids were trying to hide their drunkenness from the adults, while on the other, the adults masked their inebriation from the kids. I was in the gap between sixteen and eighteen where you can move freely between both camps, carrying the secrets of each.

I was making just such a crossing when Dad approached. He was blasted and smiling, and using that conspiratorial tone to invite me below deck to talk. I had the strong feeling that something unusual was about to happen. Not bad unusual like the old days; more interesting unusual.

He tried a couple of cabins, startling people out of quiet conversations and clandestine behavior, before eyeing the master suite at the end of the hall. Then he turned to me and asked, "Do you want to try some cocaine?"

Hell yes, I want to try some cocaine! I've been craving coke, but have never even laid eyes on it - though he clearly has. He's got a little vial with a built in spoon. I can't believe how prepared he is. My dad, the accountant, has some hardcore drug paraphernalia. And there, spilling out of the vial, is some hardcore drugs. Oh yes! He chops up the little white rocks with his platinum card and slides it into thin lines. A crisp fifty is produced. He rolls it up tight and snorts. He has a big nose. I do not. Then I get the bill, and a line of my own. The tiny room feels even smaller as I stare at the thing, secretly hoping I can do it all, so as not to seem like an amateur in front of my dad. I inhale. The coke hits my nose and the first thing to register is the smell and feel. It's chemical, not unlike bleach, which is weird because I was expecting something more like confectioner's sugar. There is no KABOOM!, though; no giant rush of feeling, and it occurs to me that I may be too drunk to feel anything more than drunk.

Dad asks what I think. I tell him quite truthfully that I like it. I'm not any higher than I was five minutes ago, but it feels good to be in the club, to be one of the guys, and to have tried such an exotic drug. And even if the effects of this drug are muted by all of the alcohol I've consumed, I still feel... like a grown up. And I want to do it again.

And two nights later, at a party on the Intercoastal, I do it again.

Sam, our host, is a huge man dressed in a black silk shirt and matching slacks. He wears a goatee and a thick gold necklace tight enough to stop the circulation to his brain. Sam is in the bar business in Ft. Lauderdale, and there are whisperings here that he is a peripheral Mafioso. He definitely looks the part and obviously wants to give the impression, but it is entirely possible that everyone just wants to know a mobster and Sam just wants to be one.

Tonight Dad and I are with his best friend and business partner, Ron. We do a quick pass through the room and suddenly we're in the bathroom knocking out lines on the back of a black toilet beneath a colorless wall-sized photo of a totally unimpressed naked woman. I wonder if I am the only person my father knows who is not in the throes of a king-sized mid-life crisis. Across from me, Ron, who I've known since I was twelve, does his line. Dad vacuums his. Then I, pretending to be a practiced hand, take the rolled up bill and go to town.

We wipe our noses and head back into the party. This time something starts to tingle in the back of my head. I feel powerful, euphoric and anxious to share my amazing personality with others. Still, I am sober enough to realize that being conversationally generous in this crowd is probably a bad idea. I'm definitely the odd boy out. I clock the average age at about forty-four, and my newly heightened powers of perception are not required to see that this is nothing like the backwoods keggers I'm used to. Everybody here has money, and lots of it. There are upturned collars, gaudy watches and soft leather loafers worn without socks. There are mini-skirts on women who seem too matronly to wear them, and hot young second wives dressing older to fit in. The music is middle class and middle aged, and largely drowned out by a fog of vodka and expensive cologne carrying tales of boats purchased, vacations taken, and financial killings made.

Our host wants to show us his 65' Vette, a black, mint-condition convertible. It is impressive. And I am easily impressed. But mostly I am craving another line of coke. I keep my mouth shut – no easy feat – and wait for the little vial to make another appearance. I could get used to this. It's fun being the rich kid partying with rich adults. But it will all end with the passing of the week. As always, I'll get back on the plane and return to Oklahoma. Dad will get busy, the goodwill will dry up, and before too long my phone calls will go unanswered and unreturned. But that's no reason to refuse a good time while it's here.

Oh Andie, what a sympathetic and believable excuse this will make if the truth ever slips out. I just wanted to bond with my dad! And this is a fact. But the far larger motivation is that I want these experiences. I enjoy getting into trouble, and this is the ultimate get out of jail free card. Professional-level shenanigans with no cost or consequence! Does it get any better than that? How can Dad, or even Mom, get mad when he is serving up the drugs, the money and even the naked women? It's not my fault! And if I am ever asked, I will hide behind the curtain of parental culpability, hoarding my high-flying memories like some vulgar treasure. Oh Andie, close your eyes, because there, in a halo of purple neon, is my apple of wisdom, and I'm definitely gonna bite. I love you. And I'm sorry. Just not sorry enough to turn around.

2

THE CHEETAH

The Cheetah III is a small building on a dirt lot in an apparent pine forest; though it's too dark to tell, especially here, by the entrance, where the lights are bright enough to get a tan at midnight. Maybe it's the narcotics or the alcohol or the giddy rush of anticipation, but I feel like we're on an island floating in the super-humid darkness. The old world ends at the road we just pulled off of, and behind that door a new world begins.

So many, many years ago when I was ten, me and Mike would steal five bucks from our moms and ride our bikes to Thomas Mall in Phoenix. The last parking lot we'd cross was the Squeeze Box, a windowless building on a busy street. "What in the hell is a squeeze box?," we would inevitably ask each other, but a sinister force field kept us from parking our bikes and actually opening the door to find out. We instinctively knew that it was better not to know, so the conversation was dropped without further conjecture. The unspoken exchange going something like, "You still don't know?"

"No."

"Neither do I."

And off we'd go to chew Kodiak tobacco and barf outside the old fashioned (even then) mall.

But here at the Cheetah III, only the specifics are in doubt. I know there's topless women in there. I just don't know what they'll look like or what the presentation will be. Maybe some older lady sauntering about with giant feathers, fans or bubbles. I've seen that on television, but it seems unlikely. The only other image I can conjure is a big stage with a sequined curtain. A three piece band is playing - a horn, a drum and a stand up bass. The musicians are blotchy, middle aged, and swollen in places that healthy people do not swell. Their souls are tired, their dreams long dead, and their performance driven by booze, amphetamines, and forty bucks a night, cash. A sweaty comedian in a twenty year-old suit introduces the girls who sashay out of the wings, spinning tassels on their bosoms. And then, I guess, they grab giant feathers, fans or bubbles and dance with them.

Okay, so I only have one idea of what a strip club might be like, and that image is melting away with every step we take toward the Cheetah III's big open door. For starters, the music coming out of the club is *Love Shack* by the B-52's, and unless Fred Schneider and the gang have hit extremely hard times incredibly recently, there is no band playing inside this bar. Again, I'm trying to act blasé, but this time for good reason. As we turn the corner I see a muscular man with puffy hair, a mustache, a starched shirt and a bow tie. No way that guy wears a bow tie out on the town. He has to be the bouncer. Gotta be mellow, act like I do this all the time.

And then, I am blindsided! All of the activity in my brain comes to a grinding halt, and it suddenly doesn't matter what the bouncer thinks of me.

I am so utterly discombobulated that I cannot for the life of me digest what I am seeing. Must breath. Try to remember how. One one-thousand, two one-thousand, "I got me a Chrysler, it's as big as a whale, and it's about to set sail!" I am vaguely aware of Dean telling the bouncer that I forgot my I.D. Three one-thousand, four, five… And finally the image is confirmed. About twenty feet inside the club, on a stage the size of a hope chest, is a completely naked woman! She has straight, black hair, kind of like Cher in the seventies. She has tan lines, kind of like my mom. Oh sweet merciful crap, please get my mom out of here! And she is wearing a gold belly chain… and nothing else.

The bouncer asks my age. I sheepishly mutter something to confirm that I am twenty-one, and a miracle happens. We get waved through. I can't believe they have a people mover in this place. Are drunks really that lazy? Oh, wait a minute, I'm walking. Must make sure. Yes, I am definitely walking. But it feels like I'm floating toward this grown up, shimmering goddess of naked womanhood. And she is dancing, but there isn't any show business to it. More like you'd dance in front of a mirror at home, if you were a little buzzed and had nothing better to do (than dance in the nude for yourself).

My heart is beating double time. And not even from sexual arousal, because this transcends sex; like finding a pirate's chest transcends money; which is, after all, just a bunch of paper with numbers printed on it. Gold, on the other hand, glitters, diamonds sparkle, and an adult naked woman's effect on a sixteen year-old boy cannot be fully described with words.

I cannot catch my breath. God, she must be 25! Older than my beloved biology teacher, Miss Maybee (whom she looks very much like). And now she is smiling at me. Naked and smiling right into my eyes. Her look says, "Take it easy, kid. It's no big deal." Easy for her to say. She has obviously never been to Oklahoma.

Okay, just smile back. Maybe it is no big deal to communicate with a naked lady; and as soon as I can get this smile squared away, I will be.

I smile. She smiles again. Then I exhale and order a Heineken because it seems like the grown up thing to do. I am in love.

***

It is a full minute and a half before I realize that there are several naked women dancing in this room. Maybe five or six at any given time on three or four different stages and tables. And I am having the most amazing run of beginner's luck, because when Cher finishes her dance, she puts her bikini back on and sits down next to me at the bar. I have totally ditched Dean. God only knows where he is or what he's doing. I'm sure I could find him if I tried, but I couldn't care less.

My conversation with Cher is brief, but eventful (for me, though doubtful for her). She asks me what I'm doing there. I tell her the truth. I'm visiting my dad for the week from Edmond, Oklahoma. "That's nice," she says.

"Do you want to go do something tomorrow? I have my dad's Porsche," I reply, desperately overselling.

"Like what?" She asks.

"We could have lunch." I pray.

"Maybe. Do you have a pen?," asks Cher.

"What for?"

"So I can give you my number," says the once and future naked woman.

I stammer something about my cursed lack of pens and she waves the bartender over and gets one from him. She writes her number on a cocktail napkin, hands it to me and says, "Give me a call." And then she is gone.

Right about now, I am beginning to suspect that I have a way with strippers. And even though I bungle the call the following day by waking her up at nine in the morning, I'm feeling oddly in my element. Like Jim Fowler must have felt the first time he wrestled a lion in the Kalahari. There is danger here, and a dark, nasty energy, but I am a big wave surfer, gliding above it all, effortlessly ducking and instinctively shifting to avoid catastrophe. Or maybe I am just drunk and full of false confidence. Either way, I'm feeling pretty damn good about it all; almost like I'm being carried along by fate.

I walk my napkin over to Dean like a war trophy. I show him the number and he pats me on the back, and remarks on my good looks. And as I'm wondering whether he was kidding, being supportive, or coming on to me, another girl approaches. This one appears to be my age. She tells me I look too young to be in this place, and asks how old I am. I lie and say seventeen. She tells me she is also seventeen. Then the drunken businessmen next to us ask her to dance for them, and as she walks away, she tells me I am cute. Three years later, when I am the muscular guy with the big hair and bow tie, I will understand that dancers are incredibly generous with compliments when farming the next ten dollar table dance. Tonight, however, I am feeling remarkably cute.

The rest of the evening goes by in a haze of AC/DC, DJ blather, and Heineken (which may be the grossest beer ever, even if it does make a high school boy feel more worldly and sophisticated). Only one more thing stands out. It is the sight of the seventeen year-old girl dancing naked on top of our neighbors' table. Her back is to me and she's spreading her legs. And though I have had sex with seven girls in my young life, it suddenly occurs to me that I have never taken a close up look at an in-person vagina, not even in my remedial attempts at going down on my girlfriends. And though I am staring, the pieces of this puzzle still aren't making any sense. It is a riddle wrapped in an enigma sealed in a paradox; an unbreakable code. And when she turns back around, and the details of her genitalia are gone, Dean asks if I want another disgusting Heineken. I nod with full sincerity. I would love another Heineken.

On the way out, I tip Cher, who is again dancing on her hope chest. I put a dollar in a garter on her thigh which is filled with money, and realize that I am eye-level with her pubic hair. I drag my gaze up to her face, and she gives me one last smile, this one a little disappointed. I promise to

13

call, and strut out like the second coming of Billy Idol. Mission accomplished.

When we get back home, Dean asks me in to the guest house to smoke a joint. He shows me a scrapbook of rock concert tickets, and shares a little story about each show. He is probably just trying to bond, but I'm more than a little paranoid that he's testing the waters for a good-night kiss. It's uncomfortable enough – or I am uncomfortable enough – that I get up abruptly and leave. He's a nice guy. Harmless. But being alone with him in a room with his bed is creeping me out in every conceivable way. I thank him and return to Dad's house.

The lights are out, and I go straight to my temporary room with the foldout couch, shut the door, and masturbate like a rhesus monkey. I pass out, exhausted, but something wakes me up about every hour or so. It's like my brain can't process all the information it has received. Or maybe it's simple guilt. I miss Andie. I miss Oklahoma. And I even miss my mom.

3

WILL ROGERS

I step off of the plane at Will Rogers Airport in a new pair of one hundred and fifty dollar ostrich skin boots. I feel ridiculous. These things don't fit right, the heel looks girly, and they cost one third of the rent my mom pays for our townhouse. They are, of course, a gift from Dad. Something I could never afford in my regular life with Mom. And, truth be told, something I would never buy for myself even if I had the money. I'll definitely wear them to school though, at least a few times, because everyone in Oklahoma wears cowboy boots, and the more exotic the creature that died for your footwear, the higher your prestige at Edmond Memorial High School.

Mom is standing in the concourse, and I am genuinely happy to see her. Ray, her live-in boyfriend of the past couple of years, is standing beside her. I have never been happy to see him. Mom is forty, attractive, physically fit and pregnant. She is an aerobics instructor and flight attendant who, like my dad, is having a bit of a midlife crisis. Her hair is frosted and she wears *Flashdance* sweatshirts that hang off her shoulder, and, in my opinion, punctuate her age.

Happily for Mom, Ray doesn't give a shit about my opinion. He is twenty-four, roughly six-two, two-sixty, with an oddly proportioned body. His arms and legs are bandy, and his torso is fat; and, because he once weighed three-seventy, his chest and back are covered in dark red stretch marks which make him look like he's been in a serious knife fight.

Ray's scars are hidden today inside of his airplane mechanic's coveralls. He works for a tiny airline based in a hangar on the runway, and is certainly only here to please my mother. He hates me and I hate him, and the only person with fantasies to the contrary is Mom.

I hug Mom and shake Ray's hand. Then he kisses my mother long enough to embarrass me and returns to his hangar on the runway.

"How was your trip?" asks Mom.

"Fine," I say, and then we are in her red Mustang with the top down in fifty-degree weather on our way back to Edmond.

4

BEAUTY & THE BEAST

I don't get my mom, and I really don't understand the Ray thing. The whole deal makes no sense at all. My dad, despite his faults, at least had something to bargain with. Ray, on the other hand, is stupid, broke, fat, and immature; even for his twenty-four years. He is also a royal fucker, though Mom doesn't seem to care. Sometimes I wonder if lying in the sun, coated in baby oil, for all these years has cooked her brain. She has always been vain; sprawling in the back of wherever we've lived in a bikini, day after day, often with her hair pulled through the tiny holes of a frosting cap, and coated with a thick, white bleaching paste, which makes her look sort of like Diana Nyad after a swim around Three Mile Island. However, two years ago, she became something else entirely; though it is possible that I'm just old enough now to see what was always there.

About a month into freshman year, I came home to find a new guy lying on Mom's blanket in the backyard. I had to squint, both from the sight of them together, and the sun reflecting off of his enormous, ass-white body. This shimmering mass of north Chicago blubber was, of course, Ray; and when he saw me standing in the doorway, he pointed – and kept right on pointing - directly at me until Mom finally got the message, and made a big motherly show of greeting me.

Right off the bat, he reminded me of an adolescent gorilla with a big Tom Cruise grin, tiny jogging shorts, and Ray-Bans; and when Mom introduced us, he bared his fangs and came in close to proclaim his dominance. I wanted to kick him in his ridiculous nuts, but he was twice my size, so instead I submitted, and went upstairs to digest this disturbing turn of events.

It wasn't a shock to have a stranger in the house; that was fairly common. And I sort of knew a fresh storm was brewing because Mom had recently brought home a bouquet of flowers from the airport. I just never would have expected this. At the time, Ray was twenty-two - eight years to the day older than me - and I could tell right away that he was emotionally unstable. For a while, I was baffled at Mom's attraction to him, but once I had a chance to think about it, I realized that he was the missing piece of a recently developing puzzle.

Mom was a high school ugly duckling who blossomed into a gorgeous swan at around seventeen, and then never really recovered from the glorious shock. The warning signs of a hardcore Cinderella complex were always there – the affairs, the obsession with appearance, the extreme identification with celebrities (Linda Evans and Farrah Fawcett, if it matters) – but when, at thirty-eight, she began to reinvent herself as the teenager she once was, the thoroughness of the project made my head spin.

For instance, one morning she woke up and announced that her name henceforth would be Carol-Anne. For as long as I could remember it was plain, sturdy Carol, but in high school guess what they called her. In her school days, she had a dog named Abear, so when our dog, Sunshine, had puppies, she kept one, named it Abear, and set Sunshine "free" in the woods. In the same fashion, her sensible Monte-Carlo vanished one night, and in its place a Mustang appeared – candy apple red and convertible, just like the car she drove in high school. Ray, of course, was the age of the guys she dated back then, and it all kept heading in the same direction.

This was happening right out in the open, which created a variety of "fitting in" challenges for Mary and me. Small town Oklahoma has some good qualities, but acceptance of unusual people is not one of them. So if your Mom changes her name, frosts her hair, buys a ragtop Mustang, and drives around town with the top down in an aerobics leotard, your friends will notice. When she joins the collagen lip injection vanguard and gets a "breast lift" (boob job), they'll recognize that too. And when a youngster moves into her room, and she claims that he is thirty and you buy it, your friends will know that you do not know.

Still, you want to give a guy a chance, especially if you're stuck with him, so I began to hover around Ray looking for things to like - or at least understand. I learned that his mother, a squat German immigrant, was a roaring alcoholic (which explained a lot), and that he had an attractive sister and a disabled brother. He also loved the Chicago Bears and seemed to be patterning himself after their quarterback, Jim McMahon. Ray had recently lost a hundred pounds, so he wore a lot of tank tops and made a habit of going to the gym. And finally, his old Nova was rusted out around the gearshift; which wasn't particularly illuminating, but you could watch the street pass by below, kind of like a glass bottom car, with shredded vinyl seats and no glass.

My research project wore on for about two months after he moved in, and once it was complete, I realized that, in addition to being young and immature, Ray was also an imbecile, buffoon, monkey boy, dickface with an incredibly short fuse. All intellectual punches had to be pulled because he was so easily stumped, and if you used words with more than two syllables, he thought you were fucking with him. He was also extremely insecure and prone to violent rages. The man was, in short, a horn-o'-plenty of things to dislike; but my least favorites were being bullied, his screaming at the television when the Bears were on, and the way he hung all over my mom.

Their game of grab ass was never ending, and there was lots of cringe-inducing making out in front of Mary and me. It was nauseating, and pretty quickly it got weird enough that Mary literally tried to choke herself to death in the middle of her seventh grade class. This move was unorthodox, but also effective, because it earned her an invitation to go back to Florida to live with Dad. Unfortunately, I was not offered the same avenue for escape, though it wouldn't have been much of one; more like a return to the sixth layer of Hell from the seventh.

Mary's departure had been in the works for a while. She was Dad's biological child, and I was adopted, so I sort of knew that if he sent a life raft to Oklahoma it would likely be a one-seater. They had also been taking private vacations lately, and he was rarely contacting me anymore. Then, when he did call, he was usually drunk in the middle of the afternoon, telling me that someone overheard a member of the Palm Beach Chamber of Commerce saying that his was the "premiere accounting firm in all of South Florida." I wanted to tell him that I was thrilled, but also still stuck with the two premiere assholes in all of Oklahoma - and maybe if there was anything he could do to help...

However, I usually didn't get a chance to speak.

5

SWEEPING DOWN THE PLAIN

Now I am in my car with Andie, and the moon is floating above the lake on one of those warm bubble nights which seems past, present, and future all at once. This is a perfect evening for parking, and she wants to get in the backseat, but as usual I can't get out of my own way. I've had a few beers and I just really need to explain *Nights In White Satin* right now.

"It's two heartbreaking things at once."

Andie gives a confused nod as I furiously wrestle momentum to the ground.

"The woman in the song is remembering nights making love in a bed of white satin while she mourns her lover, the knight, coming home from the Vietnam War in a coffin lined with white satin."

"Oh," she says, as I ramble on about the black, romantic misery of young women who hugged their men good-bye at airports like Will Rogers, only to pick them up again in flag draped wooden boxes; until Andie, the most beautiful girl in the universe, ejects the cassette, kisses me softly on the lips, and instantly shifts the charge of the atoms in the car from Moody Blues to Motley Crue. She has seen my morbidity masquerading as profundity before, and mercifully forgives it.

Our train picks up steam. There is more kissing and removal of clothing, and as Andie climbs into the backseat in her best flowery cotton panties, I am thinking, "So this is adulthood; thrilling sex with reliable frequency, and a meaningful love which lifts you high above all of life's problems... Not too shabby!"

I pull off the ridiculous boots I brought back from Florida, and join her in the back. I love her cute little belly button. I love the smell of perfume on her neck and shampoo in her hair. I love when she says my name, and I love loving her so much. I want to be with her forever, like literally every second, always. She is an angel sent from heaven, and I can't think of any other way to say it.

I take off her panties and look at her lying on the dark blue fabric in the back of my car. She is smiling and naked, and I have no memories of the past or worries about the future. There is only this perfect moment and not even music comes close to describing the feeling. I smile back, full of a calm, prayerful awareness of a God that could make such a glorious creature. Then she pulls me down on top of her and I make her pregnant.

Three months later she is gone.

6

PINK HOUSES

It's Saturday morning before the lunch rush, and the sun is streaming in the three story window in front of the food court. I'm watching the janitors clean the tables, and a few miles away, Andie is getting an abortion.

When she turned up pregnant, I was thrilled because we were going to be a family. Or at least that's how I had it planned. And because Andie broke her actual family's plan to me in stages, I had about a day to fantasize that I'd be waking up in her bed for the rest of my life, with our baby smiling between us.

As an adopted kid whose parents were constantly running away from home, I found this idea incredibly intoxicating. But for some reason, Andie wasn't interested in settling down with a sixteen year-old drunk who worked at the potato place in the mall. And her thirty-two year-old mom was even less enthusiastic.

I begged, and, regrettably, screamed at her to just have the baby and give it to me, but it had inevitably come to this; Andie, with her stepmother, in a clinic, having a sad and gruesome procedure, while I stand here making potatoes with saucy toppings for fat people who really shouldn't be eating them.

***

After work, I take her some flowers and my half of the doctor's fee. I hug her for a long time, but it isn't clear – at least to me – where we go from here. Then, inside of a month, she goes to Amarillo, and things change quickly.

My heart is breaking in a million pieces. I can't believe she's gone, and not temporarily either. Her family has moved, and they aren't coming back. I wonder if the abortion was a lie, and if perhaps she went to Texas to have the baby and put it up for adoption. It's probably wishful thinking, but they weren't moving a month ago, and I can't figure out what in the fuck is going on.

A few weeks later, Mom moves to Phoenix – where we, coincidentally, lived with Dad before he returned to Florida. This isn't really a surprise. Mom's been going to Arizona a lot lately to visit Ray at his new home. They've just had a baby, and she's starting over. I can tell she wants me to understand; like, "Come on, man, we both know this isn't working out, so let's not make it any harder than it has to be." And, to be honest, I am as happy to see them go as I was when Dad left us in Phoenix. All that tension, gone. Then the intermission where you reset the stage as the ghosts of your old life drift into the balcony to watch the rest of the show.

I get a half-hearted invitation to go with her, but I know I'm not really invited, and I wouldn't go if she got down on her knees and begged. The only chance I have of ever seeing Andie again is here, within striking distance of Amarillo, with the faint hope that she might come back some day.

Mom walks away from the house she bought less than a year ago with the settlement from her last divorce, then I am officially on my own with Abear, the family dog.

I move in with Brad, a great looking guy whose drinking makes mine seem tame by comparison. I'll be seventeen in a few weeks, but Brad may already be there. I'm not sure because there hasn't been much time for fact finding.

Brad's family took off a while ago, and he lived with a friend of ours named William, who had a terminal lung disease. I used to see those guys in the halls at school and think that they were the Lost Boys. There was probably a sense of envy too, you know, to be so free at such an early age. But because my mom was around at least some of the time, I never thought of us as being in the same boat. Now we are, though – literally.

Brad and I move into a house off the main drag. We call it our mansion, but it's really a one hundred and eighty-five dollar a month triplex next to a pawn shop. To anyone but a high school kid, this would be the worst location in town. Cars go by at all hours, there's a train track fifty yards away, and the lumber yard across the street fires up at seven in the morning. However, there is an alley over there behind a row of old brick buildings. That's where you turn when you're cruising Broadway; and that makes our red clay, postage stamp lawn the French Riviera of teenage Edmond, Oklahoma.

Overnight, we become super popular, like amusement park dwellers whose parents have died. It's crazy, and if I didn't miss Andie so much I'd be loving every bit of this, instead of, say, eighty percent.

There are genuine responsibilities too. A year's worth of screwing up has gotten me tossed out of school with less than a month to go, so now I have four hours of summer session every morning. It's the same as regular school, except that I sit next to a big guy with a beard who is twenty-five and drives a truck. He's really nice, but it scares me that I could easily be him if I don't get my act together.

By noon, class is over and my hangover has usually cleared enough to go to the gym, where I use the family membership Mom got when she was teaching aerobics. After that, I eat at Grandy's, then stick my head in our showerless tub before my shift at Wal-Mart, where I've been employed since Potatoes, Etc. fired me for some predictable accumulation of hijinks. I am a shit employee, and have already been axed from several jobs, including working in my own father's office. I will eventually be canned from this one too, but for now, I stock shelves, gather carts, and hide in the storage hall and read until nine when Wal-Mart closes. By ten, Brad and I are generally drunk again and hanging out on the lawn with the crowd that shows up after dark all summer long.

It could go on like this for years, but I'm guessing it won't because of A) our drinking, B) our love of the misdemeanor, and C) our drinking, and drinking, and drinking. All of which is complicated by our drinking, and the dark stabbing sadness that grabs me at the weirdest moments. I may be sleeping with every willing female in this stretch of the Great Plains, but since Andie left, I feel like my anchor has been cut.

It wasn't that long ago that I had family here. My grandparents lived in our apartment complex. My Uncle Tommy, who is two years older than me, was there. And my mom and my sister, Mary, lived with me full time. But now Tommy is in college, Grandma is dead, and Grandpa is freaking out in Hawaii. Mary is in Florida with Dad, and Mom is in Arizona starting a new family. I'm not related by blood to any of these people, but it never occurred to me that this mattered until they scattered so quickly with barely a wave good-bye. Andie was an island in the storm, or maybe just the faint glimmer of land in the distance. Either way, I'm drifting now, and there is only ocean and more ocean in every direction.

THE CLOUD

I drive by Andie's house so much that her neighbors probably think I'm casing the place. And if it's late enough, I'll stop and look up the hill to her window, where a "For Sale" sign loiters like an old night watchman guarding an empty vault. It's just a house – a real estate listing in a nice neighborhood in suburban Oklahoma - but it used to be the promised land to me.

On the weekends, after her parents had gone to sleep, and if I had done my begging properly, Andie would sneak me into her room. Her step dad had guns, and he thought I was the devil, so it felt legitimately dangerous and, of course, wildly romantic. I wasn't worried though, because I was Romeo and she was Juliet, and the world will always welcome lovers as time goes by – unless you are actually Romeo and Juliet, or Rick and Ilsa. Anyway, it's still completely real to me, and standing here brings it all back as clear as a bell.

Sneaky, always sneaky, I park one house down and watch for Andie to kill the porch lights. Then I sprint up the lawn like a prowler and lurk in the shrubs, waiting for her to call to me in the dark. Any neighbor looking out at this hour would logically conclude that I was breaking in, but I am incapable of rational thought. My heart is a great, glowing hippopotamus, thundering with the Vesuvian passion of young love, and all it wants in the world is to crash through her window and lie in her arms.

But there are guns, and the definite end of everything if her parents wake up and find us together. So we tiptoe, and whisper, and try to keep the covers still while we flirt with our eyes and trade baby kisses in the dark. It's like being grown ups, this laying in bed while the whole town sleeps. There is no date to go on, or parents to check in with. Just me and Andie, playing house while time stands still.

The game is always exciting, and the kissing and hugging and quiet laughing are wonderful. I love Andie, and I could do this all night, but eventually I make a trial run from first base to second. We're really past the point where this is even an issue, but once in a while she shoots me down just to keep things interesting. Happily, tonight there are no complications, and for a while I just jog back and forth, having a great time, until it occurs to me that third is probably more fun than second. So... I kind of ease over in that direction to see what's doing and linger a while in clear sight of home. I promise not to go any further, and I sort of mean it, but not really. And she doesn't believe me anyhow because this kind of promise is always a lie. Still, I keep on promising and promising until the waiting becomes unbearable.

Then, all of the sudden, we are making love, holding our breath, and listening for the faintest stirring in the kitchen down the hall. She works to keep her every sound in my ear, and it is the most beautiful music in the universe because it is proof that she thinks I'm worth the risk she's taking to have me here. I have never felt so loved in my life, or so comfortable, like half of a new person floating with the stars, a million galaxies from Oklahoma.

And then I am just me again. Sitting on a car, staring at an empty house in the middle of the night. If I don't get home soon, Brad will be screwing some poor, drunken creature on my waterbed, and I'll have to sleep where he sleeps, which is just a notch above the men's room in a bus station.

Good night, Andie, my first and only love. I miss you more than you know.

8

BOUNCING

One morning, about a month after Mom leaves, my Uncle Jimmy, a former Marine fighter pilot, and local Muzak mogul, drives down from Oklahoma City to look in on me. We talk about life and choices and the importance of direction, and then we go to a recruiter's office where I am urged to seriously consider spending the next four years living in a Quonset hut with a bunch of raging bald guys.

Jimmy is only trying to help, and my options are limited, so I try to keep an open mind during his follow-up pitch at a steak house. He is so earnest and well meaning that I am tempted join the Marines just to thank him for his concern. However, I am also one hundred percent certain that the military is not for me.

It does make me wonder, though, what is for me? I truly have no idea. I know from some of the jobs I've had, what I hate. For instance, bosses, structure, long hours, and morning schedules are big turn offs. I also know, more specifically, that food service, sod laying, paper routing, office work, door to door selling, table bussing, telemarketing, lawn mowing, elder care, janitorial labor, furniture delivery and school desk assembly are all out. I'd do any of these things again if I needed cash, but careerwise, I'd be happier as a criminal. So I make a mental inventory of my passions: Girls, rock'n'roll, weight lifting, reading, and movies. Pot smoking and beer drinking are also favorites, but I feel like I should try to be serious about this, especially if I want to be a father some day. Unfortunately, there are no obvious earners on my list, and I'm about to throw in the towel when Dale shows up with a job offer.

Concert security! Why didn't I think of that? Dale has already worked a couple of shows, and he introduces me to Ed, a skinny, chain-smoking weirdo with a darker version of my grandfather's hairdo. Ed thinks I am perfect, and hires me on the spot. Clearly he is impressed with my powerful physique, so to let him know that he has chosen wisely, I give a little flex as I pull on the ratty SECURITY T-shirt he yanks out of his briefcase. And later, when I learn that Ed's definition of perfect is someone gullible enough to let him pocket their wage, I realize that my flexing was probably very reassuring.

Ed has two accounts – rock shows and wrestling matches. The wrestling happens on Saturday mornings at The Myriad. It's a drag to get up that early, but it's four bucks an hour, cash, and you always get paid. Concerts, on the other hand, are a blast, and Ed knows it, so he promises ten bucks a night and usually pays you zero. This is fine by me because I get to stand in front of the stage and watch every radio band that comes through town over the summer. I even get to talk to a few of them, like Belinda Carlisle, who walks right up behind me on my first day, smiles, and says, "Excuse me." And Carlos Santana, who looks me in the eye after his show, shakes my hand, and says "Thank you."

Imagine that. Nobody at Wal-Mart ever thanked me for anything. Of course, I was never helpful to anyone over there, but the point is, here's Carlos Santana, one of the world's greatest guitarists, as far as I know, shaking my hand in gratitude. There is truly no business like show business, especially in Oklahoma.

Ed is a tool, but his world is so much fun, and every show is a new adventure. At a Beach Boys' concert during the seventh inning stretch of a minor league baseball game, I meet Christy, who is cute and blonde and funny. She comes back to our place that night, and we hang out off and on for the rest of the summer. And one night she calls Rock 100 THE KATT and dedicates "Take My Breath Away" to me. The deejay asks her why, and she says, "Because he's hot!," which makes me feel cooler than Matt Dillon.

One of the last shows we work is a .38 Special/Ted Nugent double bill in Norman. It rains all night, and Dale's Baja Bug, or whatever he calls it, refuses to start because the skyward exhaust is full of water. He stares gravely at the engine for about a minute, and when that fails to fix it, we sort of collectively acknowledge that we are screwed. Then, as we're plotting our next move, a girl walks by and murders my judgment in cold blood with an abrupt grab of my crotch. Her friends offer us a ride, but they aren't going anywhere near Edmond. This seems like a minor detail, so

I accept, and just like that I am on my way to Midwest City in a car full of strangers.

I wind up on the sidewalk outside of her house, waiting as she checks in with her parents. A few minutes pass, then she hops back out again through her bedroom window. She says we can't have sex, and the next thing I know we're having sex on her driveway, next to her Dad's car. As soon as it's over, she dives back through the window, and I am all alone, thirty miles from my home, in a neighborhood I've never seen before.

I start walking, though I have no idea if I'm heading in the right direction. There aren't any pay phones on this street, and there's no one to call at this hour anyway. There is, however, a full moon overhead and a black cat in my shadow, and it's really freaking me out. I cross the road to avoid the cat's path, and a pair of headlights rumble up behind me. I hear laughing, and I'm about to bolt when I realize it's Dale and Brad, come to save me.

I love my friends, I love aggressive girls, and if this job paid more than nothing, I'd do it forever.

9

WICHITA

"Did you really go to that titty bar in Florida, or did you make all that up?" Brad and I are driving to Wichita on a hot afternoon in July, and the conversation has wrapped back to the already mythical Cheetah III, as it often does when we are this drunk.

"No, I didn't go to a titty bar in Florida."

"I knew it, you fucking liar."

"Now hold on. It wasn't a titty bar I went to in Florida, it was an all nude place!" I crack up laughing because I know what's coming next.

"I hate you, I hate you, I hate you, I hate you!"

Brad is deliciously jealous, so I lay it on thick.

"Man, there was naked women everywhere. I mean I literally could not turn around without bumping into one. Hell, there must have been fifty of them."

His face lights up and he pounds on the dashboard. "That does it, when you get back from Phoenix we're going to the Red Dog!"

"The Red Dog! Like hell we're going to the Red Dog, that's a biker place. I heard you have to cover your beer over there because the dancers spray breast milk at you."

"Sold!," says Brad, and we crack up again as he opens a beer and hands me a fresh one.

I hadn't planned on drinking before the flight, but I'm off to see Mom and mixed emotions have gotten the better of me. She sent a discount ticket a few weeks ago, which is why I'm driving to Kansas to catch a plane; but the problem isn't the flight, or the drive, or even Ray, her jackass man-child. It's being alone with her that scares me.

Mom's love is a hall of mirrors, and I never know where she's coming from, or even which one she really is. She invites me to live with her in Arizona, but only when she's sure I'll say no. She lobbies for shelter from the tempers of her husbands, but instigates with impunity. And if she says she misses me, it's always with the implication that our separation is my doing. It is exhausting, and I don't want to go, but she guilted me until I agreed, then acted like she was doing me a favor. She is a master at these games, and I pity the men in her life, until I remember that I am one of them.

I wish I could explain this to Brad without sounding like a crazy person, but since that is impossible I say, "Dude, you should come to Phoenix with me." An absolutely terrible idea - he isn't packed, he's not invited, we're hammered and I'll have to write a hot check for his ticket - and still, four hours later, we stumble out of the concourse together at Sky Harbor Airport. I'm not proud of this maneuver, but if I'm going to spend three days at Mom's house, I need a buffer.

***

The first few hours at Mom's are surprisingly unhorrible. We bond over Emily, who is now four months old and unbelievably cute, and Mom politely ignores Brad's slurring and drifting in and out of consciousness. When he finally passes out, we move from the living room into the kitchen and talk while she feeds the baby. It's a good feeling, and I'm reminded how maternal she can be when there are no distractions. Ray is on his way home, so the clock is ticking, but for now it's almost like I'm four years old again and we're sitting on her bed reading books. I'm sounding out the hard words and showing her the pictures, and she's telling me how smart I am and seeming genuinely interested in the plight of a little bear or an exasperated fish. These moments are the opium dreams that force me to love her even when she's running away; and man does she always seem to be running away.

It's Phoenix now - or more specifically, Tempe - but she became an airline stewardess when I started high school, which meant living about a third of every month by myself. When the airline folded and Ray moved, she would leave town every few weeks to be with him, and before all that, we were often kept apart by strange men and circumstances. The first one I remember was the big hairy guy in Florida who used to clean our pool. She and Dad were still married, and Mom would load Mary and me into her convertible and whip us across town to his apartment. It was obvious what was happening, but at that age when you ask the big question, the subject is quickly changed.

Then after Dad left for Florida she would entertain "friends" from his office late at night, or I'd wake up and find her making out with our dentist. In pre-Ray Oklahoma, the married man who ran the gym would park two blocks away and jog over, and before that she sat me down with the guy from our apartment complex, whose windows were covered in aluminum foil, to ask if I'd mind if they commenced a sexual relationship. And while I wanted to say, "Are you people out of your fucking minds? I am failing out of the eighth grade and even I know that this is laughably inappropriate." What I actually said was, "Umm... I don't care," and that was good enough for them.

I could often hear what was going on in her room as I was trying to fall asleep, but the last thing I ever wanted was an explanation of her motivations. And yet, right after Dad left Arizona without a word to me or Mary, Mom parked me on the diving board for the first in a long and randomly occurring series of confessional monologues.

"Do you know what celibate means?" She was staring at me and picking at her bottom lip.

"Celibate?" This was early fifth grade, and while my own celibacy had been life long, I had never needed a word to describe it. "Yeah, I think so," I offered, hoping I could figure it out if she used it in a sentence.

"Well, your father and I have been celibate for more than two years and..."

Aha! Now that I had context, I realized it must have something to do with sex or not getting along, or maybe even both; which made me want to run because listening to anything in this realm felt like an Oedipal betrayal of my dad. Unfortunately, she was crying so there could be no escape. I held my breath until the subject passed, but she was just getting started. After a dramatic gaze into the middle distance, she went freeform, sharing a variety of cringe-inducing divulgences, including my father's sins while away on business trips, her ugly duckling years, her own dad's inappropriateness, the death of her first baby, and then, because she had apparently run out of things to confess, a culminating announcement of the name of my teenage birth mother. Some of this was greatest hits, but the new stuff was disorienting. And when at last she got around to the obligatory assurance that she loved me as if I was her biological child, and that sometimes she even forgot that I was adopted, I felt like I had been on a trip around the world. My head was spinning, my palms were clammy, and my chest constricted, but I was also thankful because it seemed like with Dad gone, I was being promoted to most loved and important male in her universe.

***

"Oh look, Ray is home," says Mom, and the storm clouds gather. How can she get so excited to see a man who is forever on the cusp of throwing a tantrum? Mom smiles, inviting me to smile too, but I am preoccupied with the sound of his car engine stopping, then the car door slamming, and finally the work boots on the concrete walkway. Man am I glad I don't live with them anymore. A key rattles in the knob, and Ray enters. I scan his eyes for a clue about his mood, and find that he actually seems happy to see me. But then his face crinkles in a wincing disgust. "What is that smell?"

"What smell?" says Mom.

"Holy shit - gross!" he answers, then bolts back outside to retch in the sand.

I am now officially curious, so I wander into the living room and find Brad asleep on Mom's white cloth sofa in a puddle of chunky red vomit. I try to wake him, but he just keeps on barfing. Mom's smile is gone, and she's giving me the "I am sad because you are unpredictable and totally insensitive" grimace. We, the men in her life, hate this look because it means we are irredeemable without her absolution, and it will not be forthcoming.

She is right, of course. It's my fault this time, definitely my fault. But for now, I only feel bad for Brad. How could he have known what he was getting into? And I just led him into the quagmire without so much as a change of clothes.

Oh well, at least I got to see Emily.

10

THE MAN WITH THE GUN

The other night we were out riding around and we hit a dog. We went back and found an old German Shepard dying in the grass. I was shamefully drunk, and started crying, hard, and picked the dog up and carried him back to the car. I wanted to go find its owner, but D.C. didn't want to get blood on his seats. We got into an argument and a man pulled up. I yelled at him. The guy yelled back, then we jumped in the car and chased him. We drove for about a mile, then the man screeched to a halt, turned on his hazard lights, and came charging out waving a pistol. He was aiming the gun at us and making threats, until he saw the blood on my shirt and asked what the hell was going on. I pointed to the dog in the backseat. Then he looked me in the eye, sneered, and got back in his car and left.

I'm afraid I'm losing control. I love to get fucked up and I love the way my heart pounds when I'm stealing gas or beer, or just sneaking around, causing trouble after curfew. But my lack of fear, and disregard for authority is scaring me. The well-meaning adults who used to try and help have all stepped aside, died, or left town, and it seems like no one says no to me anymore. The girls who come over are looking for a bad boy, so I don't even have to try with them, and the guys defer because I am the only one, other than Brad, who doesn't have to listen to his parents. I like it, I really do. But I've been lucky so far, and I know it won't last. Maybe it will be some girl's boyfriend or father. Maybe it will be the cops who seem to drive past our door every couple of hours. Maybe some of those kids from other towns will drift across the street from the parking lot where they hang out. Or maybe I'll just drink too much and not wake up. Who knows.

There's always a tornado coming in Oklahoma, especially in the summer, and I've been out in the field begging it to hit me. Now I'm scared.

11

OKLAHOMA

There is another reason, aside from Andie, that I want to stay in Oklahoma. I love this place. It's not much to look at; lots of red mud, brown trees, rolling hills and harsh wind, but it is beautiful to me. I don't take it for granted either. A hell of a lot of things had to break right for me to get back here, and I don't ever want to leave again.

I was born in Oklahoma. And because I am my entire family tree, biologically speaking, I think of it as the other half of me, like the soil that hides my roots. Out here, my history could be anywhere. Every face could be a relative, and every place could be home. It is a gigantic mystery, but a generally comforting one.

Oklahoma, and particularly Edmond, has also been a big source of stability. My mother is a gypsy and my father is a careerist, so we have always moved at the drop of a hat. We left here when I was two, and by the time I returned to live with my grandparents at the beginning of the eighth grade, we had already lived in Ft. Lauderdale, Boca Raton,

Miami, Phoenix, then back to Boca again. And in the three and a half years that Mom was here, we lived in seven different places just in Edmond.

The traveling actually started for my mother and me even before she married my dad. My mom's teenage marriage ended when her baby died of a genetic disorder. There was a fifty-fifty chance that any child she and her husband conceived would be born with the same condition, so they adopted me and moved to The Bahamas to start over. A few months later, husband number one was gone for good, and Mom and I were back in Oklahoma, where she left me with her parents and started trying to put her life back together. She already knew my dad, who, as fate would have it, had gone with her to the hospital to bring me home for the first time. They got married shortly after reconnecting, bought a house in Oklahoma City, sold it, and we became situational nomads.

The constant in all of this was our annual trips back to Oklahoma to see my grandparents and Tommy. They lived in an apartment complex that bordered a cow pasture on one side, and an endless, overgrown field on the other. You could spend all day out there exploring the trails in the waist high grass, and there was no end to the treasures you would find. Old couches, rotting lumber, dirty magazines, abandoned appliances, cigarette butts and hobos, all in a picturesque nature setting. And when you'd had enough high adventure, you could walk to a hamburger joint where you ordered by calling the kitchen from the phone at your table. There was family to visit, a swimming pool, trips to the public golf course, and a 7-Eleven where you could win a Slurpee by dropping a penny into a shot glass at the bottom of a pickle barrel full of water. It was paradise, and when my parents' second marriage to each other blew up in Boca Raton, I got a chance to live in Edmond permanently (or as permanent as it ever got).

Just prior to my return to Oklahoma, we were living in Arizona. We'd been there for about four years – two with Dad, and two without – when my parents decided to reconcile. It was a startling announcement, and they moved fast to keep from losing momentum.

You don't really get used to pulling up stakes this much, but the markers on the road get familiar. Almost the instant you hear the news of relocation, your old life starts to deflate. People drift away and everything takes on an aura of impermanence. A sign goes up in the yard, your belongings get stuffed into boxes, and strangers start wandering through your bedroom. If the end of a school year is close, as it was for me this time, fear of the lonely unknown increases in direct proportion to everyone else's happy anticipation of summer vacation. You listen to their plans and know they won't include you, ever again. Then, eventually, you just accept what is happening and get used to being a ghost.

This time, I didn't have to stay until the very last day of school, so there was no climactic final bell and no giddy crowd to wade through. Just a quick glance back at the seventh grade as I climbed into the car and drove across the country to move in again with Dad.

It was a shaky situation from the start. Dad was trying, and so was Mom, but even at thirteen I could tell this wasn't going to work any better the second time than it had the first. Dad was still gay, Mom was still Mom, and to ensure disaster, Dad invited his mother down from Dallas to move into the guest house.

Grandmother was rustic Oklahoma by way of agrarian Texas; the kind of woman who gets called Grandmother because Grandma is too familiar. She was abrupt and frugal, and unpretentious enough to leave her dentures and prosthetic mastectomy breast in the closet when she didn't have somewhere to go; all of which fed a simmering tension between her and my parents.

With the trip back to Florida, Mom was re-imagining herself as the Linda Evans of Boca (from the Farrah Fawcett of Phoenix), and some of the pieces actually fit. She had a tropical home in a genteel neighborhood, fashionable clothes, a nice car, a swimming pool, and a husband with his own firm. But in the middle of it all was Grandmother, with too few teeth and boobs, shuffling around in a housecoat and loafers, stringing lines of decades old underwear from her house to ours. These women would never, under any other circumstance, have chosen each other's company, and they were held together by a man, my father, who clearly wanted to get the hell away from both of them.

My parents' personal and sexual incompatibility was as obvious as our next-door neighbor's toupee, and try as he might, Dad couldn't do anything to make his marriage more authentic or his mother less miserable. So he gave up - quickly. He would come home from work, walk straight to his bedroom, emerge to eat dinner, and then sit at the table smoking cigarettes and mashing them out in his plate while Grandmother read aloud from the most morbid stories in the paper.

Things got dark. Dad would smile and be horrible at the same time. Mom looked the other way. I didn't realize what was happening at first. He'd been gone for a couple of years, and I'd only really seen him once between the fifth and seventh grades. The jokes on the drive from Phoenix to Florida were probably my first clue. When we were alone he'd start, and initially I thought, "Cool. Dad's humor is kind of creepy and graphic, but maybe this is him reaching out." Soon though, the jokes stopped feeling like jokes. More like a warning, or a sign of things to come. And right around this time, he asked me, "Have you ever had a blow job?" I hadn't, and I was waiting for the punch line, but it never came. By then – maybe a month after our arrival back in Boca – he had already started busting into my room, always laughing and smiling, trying to shove his fingers up my ass. These moments would happen fast. Almost like he was checking to make sure he could still do it. And I was resisting and basically being overpowered, but I didn't know what to make of it, or even what to call it. I knew I didn't like it, and it wasn't funny to me, but at least initially, there was nervous laughter as I tried to get my face to match my feelings, and figure out what was going on.

There was nowhere to hide. Dad could be in and out, so to speak, in twenty seconds, and Mom and Mary were often just in the other room. Basically, if he was home, there was a pretty good chance it was coming. I wanted to get away, but I didn't know anyone yet, so I wandered the neighborhood looking for other kids; hopefully ones with pot and alcohol connections.

Eventually, I found some long-haired high-schoolers hanging out on a lawn. One of them had a VW Bug, and for a small tax he would drive you into the black neighborhood to buy nickel bags of weed from the young men who sold out of their front yards. After about a month, I got brave enough to ride my bike over there, and the only problem I ever had was deciding who to buy from.

I was barely thirteen, and my new drug friends were two or three years older. I doubt if they even knew my name, so until I met the younger guys, I tried to be quiet and just observe. There was a girl who seemed intelligent, and a guy who seemed volatile. There was a tall, funny kid too, who once told me that he had fucked the girl, "If you consider two inches of a twenty-five inch cock a fuck." In this crowd, my only real drawing card was the money I made filing in my father's office, and I was beginning to get taken advantage of when Dan and Bob came along. They were satellites to the older kids, and I was more than happy to leave the mother ship and join them in their less illustrious, but far more comfortable, orbit.

Dan was a skinny eighth grade surfer who lived with his Dad. And Bob, also an eighth grader, effectively lived alone with his sixteen year-old sister because his mom had an offsite boyfriend. Our connection was getting high, and we did basically everything in our power to stay that way. When our beer and dope ran out we would smoke bong resins or steal liquor from our parents, and when that dried up we'd sniff gas fumes from the older kids' mopeds or knock each other out playing choking games. We were committed to the cause, and personal safety was not a huge priority.

My new friends were a relief, but the wackiness at home continued. Right before school started, Tommy came down for a visit. The day before his arrival, Dad pulled me aside and said, "Let's not tell Tommy how we play," which might have been the most frightening moment in the whole ordeal. It wasn't like I didn't know something was wrong, but this was almost a Presidential proclamation that, "This is happening!" And furthermore, it signaled that he knew what he was doing and intended to keep on "playing" when Tommy left. Mom knew it too. One morning she saw me running out of his room pulling up the back of my pants, and she said, "What's going on?" Dad grinned, and she left it at that. Another time they came home drunk. I was lying on the floor in their room watching the only television in the house, when they stumbled in laughing. Dad grabbed my legs and started trying to stick his fingers in my ass through my underwear. I managed to get away, but there was no follow up from Mom.

It was scary, and also confusing because if you took away the repeated attempts at digital penetration, and the constant, leering double-entendres, sometimes it seemed like I had jumped from the least favorite person in the family to Dad's numero uno. He would tell me that he couldn't imagine a better son, and other things along these lines that he'd never said before. It wasn't necessarily believable, but it was more than enough to befuddle.

Near the end of the summer, I went to Mom and asked her if Dad was gay. She said yes, and sort of looked off in space. There was no talk of what to do now, just a melancholy, distracted "Yes," and that was that.

A month later, I started the eighth grade, and made it about five weeks before I was thrown out of class for goofing around. On the way out the door, I got caught trying to pass my cigarettes to another kid. The principal called my parents and suspended me for a week. Dad came home from the office and took my shoes so that I couldn't go anywhere. He was seething, and I knew he meant business, but when Bob came by on his bike an hour later and asked if I wanted to go and score some pot, I didn't really consider saying no. I thought for a moment about Dad. How much madder could he realistically get? He had taken my guitar away a few weeks prior and when I'd raised it to strike him, he covered his head and ducked. It was reflex, and I had no intention of swinging, but that moment was a revelation. It scared the shit out of me that I might already be able to scare him, though the thought gave me courage as I considered Bob's invitation. I wanted to get high. I was sick to death of this situation. Dad had recently tackled me coming out of the shower, reached up under my towel and grabbed my balls. This time I screamed, "Stop!" And once he had succeeded in his mission, he did stop. Then he got up, walked into his bedroom, sat on the sofa, and grinned at me as I passed through from the bathroom like, "You are zero, and I own you." I just didn't see how it could get any worse. So, feeling like I had nothing to lose, I jumped on Bob's handlebars and rode off into the afternoon.

We spent the rest of the evening hanging out with the other stoners, who were all kind of amazed at the trouble I had gotten myself into. I should've been scared, but even sitting there in my bare feet, with no money in my pockets and no one to really turn to for help, I felt like I was in a protective bubble. I'd thrown myself at the mercy of fate, a far heavier authority than my parents, and it was pretty much up to her how this all turned out.

I didn't worry until ten o'clock, when it was time to go home. Bob rode me back to my house and dropped me at the hedge by the street. Fearing fireworks, he cleared out quick, and I stood alone in the damp courtyard for what seemed like an hour, but was probably just a few seconds. Since I didn't have a key, I walked to the oversized door and knocked. There was clattering in the hall, and Dad answered, holding my shoes. Before I could speak, he told me in an angry whisper to leave and meet him at his office on Monday morning. Then, without waiting for a response, he shut the door, and it was just me and the lizards skittering across the moldy bricks.

I pulled on my shoes, took my bike from the garage, and rode the three miles to Bob's place. As usual, his Mom was gone, so he and his sister took me in.

Bob's house was basically his to do with as he wished, but I didn't envy his freedom. His home was like a squatters' hovel with too little structure and too much space. There was nothing in the kitchen, nothing on the walls, and no adults around to give a shit. There were mattresses in their bedrooms, but Bob and his sister usually slept on the floor in the living room; and for the next few days, so did I.

In the morning, we found a lawn mower in the shed in their overgrown backyard, and we pushed it around the neighborhood trying to get someone to pay us to trim their grass. Eventually, we succeeded and made enough money for noodles and a nickel bag of weed. This felt like the pinnacle of the day until Bob's sister's friend came over and pretended to be asleep for about a half an hour while me and Bob felt her boobs.

The pot didn't last long, though, and neither did the boobs, so we mostly sat around all weekend doing nothing. Then on Sunday evening, a former boyfriend of Bob's mom, who may have been paying the rent, stopped by. When he found an extra kid in the living room, and learned that I was essentially a runaway, he wanted to call my parents. I thought about this for an instant and then bolted for the door, jumped on my bike, and hauled ass to Dan's house.

Dan's father was a good man. I was obviously trouble, but he took me in anyway and let me stay the night. In the morning it was left up to me how to proceed.

The rain was coming down in buckets, and school was about to start, so Dan's dad offered to take me home or loan me some clothes if I wanted to go to class. I decided to stick with the original plan and go to my dad's office, as instructed. I rode about four miles in a downpour to the converted mansion that housed my father's firm, and got there before anyone else arrived. Dad met me at the door, led me into his office, and parked me in the chair in front of his desk. He then took his seat before the big picture window that looked onto a small garden, and gave me two choices. Either I could go to military school in South Carolina or I could move to Edmond and live with my grandparents and Tommy.

It was still raining, but it seemed like the clouds had parted and the sun was shining directly on me. Could this really be happening? Was I really being offered the chance to live in Oklahoma? Alone? With no hectic family situation? I tried to play it cool because I was afraid that if I seemed too eager, he would take it back. I let the word Oklahoma drift past my lips with as much nonchalance as I could muster, and when he said "Okay, you leave tonight," I felt like angels were picking me up and flying me to the promised land.

***

And just like that, I am on a plane in a storm with my mother. She orders a small bottle of wine, and while she is in the bathroom, I finish it. A two sentence interrogation follows. I lie, she scowls, then we bounce through the air and land in another heavy rain.

It's almost midnight when we touch down, and all I can see are the warning lights shimmering off the tarmac, and the terminal glowing in the distance. But while the hour and the unknown are spooky, I feel free because I am sort of on my own now – or will be shortly – and there is really nothing left to lose.

At the gate, Grandma, Grandpa and Tommy are waiting, their forced frowns becoming guarded smiles. Clearly, my new reputation precedes me, but I am excited to see them, and speeding up to close the gap when Mom musters her trademark scene stealing tears. Argh! Upstaged in my own play - again. She is a Jedi master of these dramatics, and they nearly always work like a charm; in this case to preemptively change the subject from "Failed Parent" to "Cruel Child."

So I wait through the comforting of my mom by her mom, and when it is done my grandparents turn and remark on how skinny I've gotten. Their concern is sincere, but tinged with, "Don't you see how this hurts your poor mother?" No, not really. I have honestly never considered my weight, or the effect it may have on others. Later, though, after showering, I get on the scale. At thirteen, I am 5'10, 105 pounds, literally soaking wet. Which seems like a fine starting point for a journey of... eating, I guess.

For now, though, I can live with skinniness because my escape is complete. And in the morning, I get to go to Sequoyah Middle School on Danforth Road, over by the graveyard. I honestly can't wait, and the only drawback is the tone in the working class townhouse of my childhood vacations, which has changed. The suspicion is palpable, and even Tommy - a straight-A sophomore with coke bottle glasses, braces and a longish bowlcut - seems leery. My time with him will be monitored, and there will be occasional "We're on to you," style comments. Over the next couple of months, my mother's sisters will appear, each pulling me aside for a "Don't you even try it..." lecture. Of course, I will try it, often and with relish, but they will never know the half of it. Sermons rarely work. But a change of scenery can, and already has. This is home now (and again), and the relative stability and happy history are enormously reassuring. I also know that despite their wariness, my grandparents really do love me. They are just scared. My aunt's first husband died of a drug overdose in his early twenties, and I think they are frightened that the same might happen to me. There is also a heavy history of alcoholism among the men in our family, and everyone has lived through their share of trouble and heartbreak. So I understand, at least partially, the hesitation everyone's feeling. And whether that part of it bothers me or not, this situation is obviously a million percent better than the one I was living in just a few hours ago. And, of course, best of all, here is Oklahoma, at last, where tornados may prowl, but the ground never shifts.

I fall asleep that night across from the enchanted dumping ground, and within earshot of the mooing of cows. A pack of cigarettes I will never finish is tucked under my pillow, and there is an ease in my spine and stomach because Mom is leaving in the morning. Finally, I am where I belong. And though this arrangement isn't supposed to be permanent, there is no way I will ever live in Florida again. No fucking way.

12

AMARILLO (PART 1)

Something is wrong. I feel sick and in a strange position, and there is the vague sensation of movement. There is also talking, and an unfamiliar deejay on a radio playing just loud enough to annoy. I hope this is a nightmare, but I've never felt like throwing up in a dream.

I open my eyes and realize that I'm lying on someone's shoulder. It's Reid, a fifteen year-old boy who's been hanging around with us lately. I still don't get it though. I want to stretch my legs, but I can't because I'm in the backseat of my car. I check up front. Brad is driving, Dale is riding shotgun, but where are we going?

Dawn is about to break, and through the bug-splattered windshield I see streets signs, but don't recognize the names... Or the streets, for that matter. And then, like a lightning bolt, a vicious pang of memory zips through me. Quick flashes of last night whirl past. I'm crying on the phone, I'm making an announcement to the crowd which seems to appear like cockroaches in our living room the instant the sun goes down; and then I'm standing in the breakdown lane on I-35 throwing up in the weeds by Frontier City. If all of this happened, and it sure smells like it did, then I'm pretty sure I know where I am, and it is not good.

I say the first words that come to mind; "Please God, tell me we're not in Amarillo, Texas." Brad and Dale bust up laughing, and then it all comes back to me.

Yesterday, Brad and I threw a couple of cases in the trunk and drove out to the country to cut loose. He said there'd be girls out there, but by the time we arrived everyone was gone, which was unsurprising because Brad is the king of overselling a party. We still had beer, though, and the radio in the car, and a relaxing location in which to drink ourselves blind, so that's exactly what we did.

This was all pretty normal stuff, but here lately, my obsession with Andie is all consuming – and it grows with every beer I drink. I just can't shake the idea that maybe the abortion was a lie. They left so soon afterward, and with so little notice, that, at least mathematically, anything is possible. I think, maybe she went down there to have the baby and put it up for adoption; and perhaps she doesn't want to give it up but her parents are forcing her. And if that's true, then there might still be time to stop it if I can find them.

For most of the summer, all I've known for sure is that they are in Amarillo, but a few days ago a letter came; and with it, her return address and telephone number.

I had no idea why she was suddenly sharing this information with me. Her parents had insisted on a clean break, and aside from a couple of quick phone calls, she had complied. So, since it wasn't cool to just pick up the phone and dial, I began to see this letter as a seed; and if it was ever going to come to fruition, I would need patience, restraint and maturity at levels far beyond my current capacity – which was zero. I resolved to cultivate this opportunity like a bonsai tree; carefully tending and pruning as I made similar modifications to my own character. Then, as my sapling and I grew into appropriately formed organisms, I could use my newfound serenity to reconcile with Andie, and stop her parents from giving our child to some stranger without my consent.

Unfortunately, I made this resolution on Tuesday, and here I am on Sunday, waking up drunk in a moving car, two hundred and fifty miles from home, en route to a showdown with her family over this incredibly sensitive issue.

I am not stupid, though; and once in a while, during a lonely moment pushing a broom in the outer reaches of Wal-Mart, it occurs to me that a drunken monkey with a loaded pistol would make a better dad for this baby - which likely no longer exists - than I would. But how do you tell someone you care about that they are inadequate, especially when that someone is you? I want so desperately to be a father, but there is just no evidence that I am ready to have my own family. I drink more beer than the crowd at an 89er's game, Brad and I keep track of the girls we fuck on a scoreboard (with an embarrassing number of duplicate entries), and my efforts as a vandal and thief far outpace anything I've done to prepare myself for parenthood.

I can see all of this, but only in flashes. And in these moments, I get it. You shouldn't pull a train, even if the girl wants you to. You shouldn't shoplift, and if you're going to, you definitely shouldn't try to prove your bravery by screaming, "Wahoo!" on the way out of the store. And why steal just to steal? Brad has a Wall Street Journal newspaper machine in his room, and I have a huge banner on my wall proclaiming "He is risen!" We don't need these things. To the contrary, if our refrigerator weren't overflowing with purloined beer, then we wouldn't have increased our nightly capacity from eight to ten, and then from twelve to fourteen, and now from eighteen to twenty-four. And I definitely wouldn't be waking up in Texas with barf on my jeans.

A wise man would absolutely stop right now and cut his losses. He would go back to Edmond and beg the forgiveness of his family, friends, townsfolk, and municipal officials. He would acknowledge his shortcomings and realize that there is no way to make a good impression when you reek of stale beer and fresh vomit. And a wise man would also understand that even if he was miraculously given the power to overcome the well-founded objections of her loved ones and his teenage drinking buddies, suddenly being married with a child wouldn't change a thing.

But I am not a wise man. As a matter of fact, I am no man at all. I am seventeen years old, and these decisions are too painful to make, so I will continue on to Andie's house with the very slim hope that love can conquer all, and let life decide my next move for me. This is the coward's way out, but I love her with all of my heart and that is the only thing I have in the world right now.

13

AMARILLO (PART 2)

I'm here. But now what? Not only am I uninvited, I have specifically been told twice in the past twenty-four hours not to do this. Last night Andie said, "Don't you dare come to Texas!" And this morning when I called from a roadside motel, she said her parents weren't going to let her see me even if I showed up at their door. But here I am anyway, standing in the super bright sunshine, staring at a small townhouse with a flat brown yard. It looks temporary, and maybe it is. However, there is no doubt that I'm in the right place, because there's her car and the address matches the letter I'm holding.

So it's high noon at the O.K. Corral – except that it's seven in the morning and my only real opponent is me. I'm terrified. I can't do this alone. Damn it, why don't they just come out here and give me something to react to? The cowards! They're probably scared shitless. I know I am. What in the fuck am I doing in Texas on a Sunday morning, anyway?

I catch my reflection in their picture window and can't believe what I see. Who is this rumpled, bloodshot person, and what can he possibly have to say for himself? He loves this girl, but it's selfish, the way a baby loves its mother; without perspective, and clouded in fear of everything else in the world.

Dear God, what a terrible time for a moment of clarity.

I am, however, still moving toward her door. And after this season of anguish, I'm finally just a few feet from the girl I love and the answers I've craved. All I have to do is knock.

But I can't. Not now. I mean, look at me. I'm Dr. Jeckyll and Mr. Hyde; and let's be honest, mostly Mr. Hyde. I want a baby so badly. I want our baby. But would a real father want me to raise his child? Not anymore than you'd want a hulking, retarded Lenny to raise your rabbits. My legs buckle, my stomach drops, and it occurs to me that now would be an excellent time to quit telling myself stories about starting a family. These ideas are only romantic to a point, and when you wind up in Amarillo, Texas with barf on your jeans, maniacal desperation in your eyes, and three other guys in your car, the romance has officially left the building.

I plod back to the car, and already everything seems different. There is an overpowering stench of sour alcohol, which I cannot believe I didn't notice before, and my friends, who were laughing their asses off an hour ago, seem ashamed. It's hard to tell if it's my shame they're experiencing or some of their own, but everyone clearly understands that we have pushed this too far (a brand new sensation for us all). And then there is the car itself, with its louvers and bra and massive Firebird decal. I've been so enamored of this machine, but it suddenly reminds me of an Evel Knievel bicycle I had in the second grade.

Once upon a time, my Evel bike's plastic gas tank and stars and bars motorcycle fenders made me so proud. Then one day I was cruising along and it hit me that I was riding a stupid little kid's toy with a lot of superfluous shit on it. I was mortified, like in those dreams where you get to school and realize you've forgotten to wear pants. I thought about ditching it in the bushes and telling my parents it got stolen, but instead I rode straight home and pulled off all of the fake motorcycle crap. Underneath was just a plain white bicycle, but at least it wasn't a baby's toy.

***

We ride back to the interstate in silence. It's already scorching hot and we're sweating like vampires who've lost their coffins. Everyone we pass seems to be on their way to church, and I want to duck beneath the dashboard and hide my face from this ungodly light.

I really shouldn't be driving. Exhaustion and fear of the unknown have me feeling like a stranger in my own skin; and then there is this world-class hangover. My skull is pounding, I'm going to puke, and a two-word sentence is spinning through my mind like a rocket fueled merry-go-round, "Everything counts." No shit, everything counts. You're telling me everything counts? Of course everything counts. The plains stretch out forever, and everything counts. You can't get away with anything because everything counts. Here you are because everything counts, and you'd better know what you know, because every last thing you do in this world counts – forever.

Man, I really, really, really shouldn't be driving.

14

THE ROAD HOME

"Are you alright?"

There is a frightened woman standing over me and the tidal whoosh of cars flying past in opposite directions. I've only been out for a few minutes, but I am extremely disoriented. This lady wants an answer, and I want to calm her down, but for the life of me I can't remember why I'm sleeping in the median on the highway.

"I'm fine," I mumble, and she looks at me like I'm a crazed degenerate; which I sort of am. And now I'm a little annoyed. I mean, can't a guy get a little privacy in the middle of the interstate without the whole fucking world demanding an explanation?

Wait a second. It's coming back to me now. I let Reid drive because no one else wanted to. He's fifteen, so I was sort of giving him a driving lesson as I drifted off. Then, a few minutes later, I woke up to the sound of my engine blowing up. Apparently, the transmission was slipping and Reid was trying to accelerate through, and now we are stranded outside of Groom, Texas, in sight of the – no joke - tallest cross in the Western Hemisphere.

Truth be told, Brad and I are the only ones presently stranded. Reid and Dale have walked back toward the cross to find someone to give us a tow, and I, being too nauseated to accompany them, am trying to get some rest in the median because the car is so uncomfortable.

The lady storms back to her Pontiac, clearly furious with me for scaring her. And the feeling is mutual, because waking up with a panicky stranger in your face is jarring, to say the least. But now, like a normal distressed motorist, I've got to stay awake or people will keep pulling off the road and demanding answers. I sit on the hood and stare at the massive cross for a while, but it is so on the nose I can't bring myself to read anything into it. And besides, everything from Texas to Nebraska is church country, so the only thing unusual about this sight is its enormity; like seeing a beer stein the size of an office building at Oktoberfest.

I get back in the car and sweat like a pig. The radio reception is spotty, so my choices are Sunday morning religious broadcasts or the sound of Brad snoring. I choose the snoring and the traffic, and the hyper-critical pleadings of my incessant conscience. It didn't used to run on like this, but since Mom left, I've been plagued with this horrible feeling of responsibility for my own behavior, which always hits hardest the morning after I have done something remarkably stupid. My conscience used to be a silent observer of my idiocy; or at worst, a disapproving old lady shaking her head on the porch across the street. But now I'm trapped with Mr. Smith, in full-throated filibuster, all day, every day. Beer turns it off for a while, but it only comes back louder in the morning.

The bad old days were heaven. I was so comfortable raging against the machine. The self-righteousness was amazing, and it fit me like a glove. But now that the machine is gone, my raging just feels like raging. And it isn't just because Mom left. Whether the baby still exists or not, the ramifications of the pregnancy are impossible to ignore. Who would I be rebelling against if there were a tiny person to care for? I can't come up with an answer for that, and thank God I don't have to, because at last there is a tow truck pulling onto the grass behind us.

The truck is newish and the man driving it is old. His name is Jack Bivens, and two things are clear the instant he lays eyes on me: He has heard the story of why we are lost in Texas on the Sabbath, and he is totally unsurprised that I am the jackass in charge of it all.

Jack is short and bandy. His uniform is worn, but well laundered, and may have even been pressed. He exudes competence, doesn't talk much, and seems to see right through me. Now here is someone I can read into. His diagnosis is not good. The engine is gone, and he'll have to send away for a new one. He can probably do it on the cheap by salvaging a motor from a junkyard, but that will take a couple of weeks at least, and he is wisely insisting on payment in full before starting the job. So, since "on the cheap" still means fifteen hundred dollars, I'll have to call one or both of my parents in their states of residence before anything can happen with my car in Groom.

As fucked as I was an hour ago, to be only that fucked once more would be a dream come true. I have zero dollars in my pockets, and the combined wealth of my three friends wouldn't buy a chicken fried steak at Braum's. The only thing any of us has to fall back on is my checkbook, and it would be a miracle if there were ten bucks in the account. But, any port in a storm.

We leave the relative comfort of Jack Bivens' shop and start walking. He has phoned Greyhound and arranged for the Oklahoma City bus to pick us up on the highway. We can pay the driver with a check and worry about how to make it good later. This sounds more than fair to me, but now there are six hours to kill in Groom and nowhere to hide.

Everywhere we go for the rest of the day, the eyes of Texas are upon us. We eat at the diner, where hot checks are obliviously accepted, and people gawk. We walk toward the underpass and they come to their windows to watch. We wait and sweat, and sweat and wait, and the local sheriff drives by at least a half a dozen times staring the timeless stare of the lawman who knows that people are rotten but cannot yet charge them with anything.

Then, at long last, the Greyhound appears on the horizon. My heart speeds up as the bus slows down, and I can almost feel the air conditioning and the big comfortable seat. I pull out my checkbook and get ready to take a nap, but as I reach for the door the driver picks up speed. Can this really be happening? I hope not, but I recognize the look on his face as the one we've been getting all day long. A half a second later, it is clear that we have been ditched by Greyhound. I understand why, but sweet mother of sweetness, who do you turn to when Greyhound won't pick you up?

Brad and I go for each other's throats. He blames me, I blame him, and we carry on like a couple of full-blown morons accusing each other of being stupid. We are, in fact, so consumed with our squabble that we fail to notice a minor miracle occurring just a few yards away. Near the beginning of our debate, Reid stuck his thumb out and two girls in a truck stopped and offered us a lift to White Deer, Texas. White Deer is in the wrong direction, but I'm ready to accept just to get off this road; and the deal gets sweeter. They're going to Oklahoma in the morning, and if we can make a good impression on their parents, we can ride back home with them.

My breath would make a homeless man blanch, I haven't showered in days, and I've just lost pretty much everything in the world that matters to me, but I'm still thinking that if all I have to do is charm a couple of rednecks, we're probably home free.

This hubris is astonishing, particularly in light of my recent history, but a number of factors have suddenly swung in my direction. The wind is blowing the puke stink off of my clothes, sweating all day has settled my stomach, and I am wearing a relatively clean pair of boxer shorts.

A lesser mind might ignore the problem solving capacity of his underwear, but not me. Every girl in school wears boxers as if they were regular shorts. Hell, my mom does it. You just sew up the front and BAM!, perfectly good short pants. So if I just take off my unspeakably rank jeans and go in my unmentionables, maybe I can convince these girls' parents that I am a clean-cut kid having a little run of bad luck (after driving drunk to Texas in the middle of the night for perfectly wholesome reasons). It's a bit of a long shot, but it could work. However, for a plan like this to succeed you need one hundred percent faith in its foundational logic.

Is it okay to walk into a stranger's home in your underwear?

Absolutely, as long as you believe in your heart that your underwear is not underwear.

Is it okay to lie in order to get yourself and your friends back home?

No, you shouldn't lie to helpful people, so I will tell a PG version of the truth and hope for the best.

And finally, is it okay to pretend to be something you're not?

You mean a good person? A blameless victim of circumstance? Someone who actually deserves help?

This is where my scheme falls apart. And at the worst possible moment.

It's show time, and I'm sitting on a plastic covered couch in a tidy mobile home on a gravel lot, facing down a large man in a John Deere cap and his matronly wife - in my underpants. I've offered them a completely sincere, though slightly varnished, recounting of events, but they're still giving me the bus driver's stare. I am dying the death, and everything I try just makes my flop sweats more pronounced. I resort to lying, my conscience screeches, doubt creeps in, and as my shorts turn back into underwear, the whole summer flashes before my eyes. Then the last year and a half with Andie, and finally the sickening realization that I am really, no kidding around, going to have to beg my parents for mercy.

I throw in the towel and ask permission to make a long distance call. Mr. Deere motions me to the kitchen phone, while his wife keeps Brad pinned to the couch with a barrage of pointed small talk. My hubris is long gone, and I feel like the Wizard after Toto pulls back the curtain, except that no one but me thought I was the Great and Powerful Oz. I am a stranger without pants. A dunce with no money. I am completely free, but only because I've lost everything. And I am a coward to boot, because I know the funds to fix the car will have to come from Dad, but I'm phoning Mom because he is the world heavyweight champion of tearing a person down to nothing when they are at their most vulnerable; and he almost never takes my calls.

I dial, Mom answers, and I speak in an even hush because the Deeres are tracking my every move. My mouth goes dry. I don't know where to begin, so to remind myself that life goes on outside of this conversation, I watch Dale and Reid – who weren't among the lucky two allowed inside – as I get to the heart of the matter.

"Um, Mom, my car broke down."

"Oh, no."

"Yeah, and it's going to cost about fifteen hundred dollars to fix."

"Oh, dear."

"Yeah, and um, I'm in Texas.

"You're in Texas! Why?"

"Andie."

"What about Andie?

"Well, I think she had an abortion. But then I didn't think that anymore, and I got worried and came out here -"

"Damn-it, why don't you leave that poor girl alone!"

"What?"

"This is so irresponsible, you can't just…"

"Wait a second…"

"We don't do this, okay. We just don't do this!"

"Um… Look, say no if you have to, but I'm not sure what "we" you're talking about." My volume increases. Mr. Deere sits up in his chair.

Mom continues, "I am talking about our family, okay! And our family does not do this kind of thing."

"What family!"

Mr. Deere stands, Brad shakes his head for me to please, please cool it; and I want to, but I'm speeding toward a cliff with no brakes.

"So now you want to be a parent? Now you want to put me down and give advice? Well where were you when I needed to talk? Where were you ever!"

Suddenly, I am a fly on the wall, watching a kid sobbing and pacing in the kitchen of two good people who woke up this morning anticipating church and football, and wound up entertaining an interloper's soap opera.

"Fuck you, Mom! I hate you!"

She's yelling back at me, but I can't hear what she's saying, and I'm not exactly sure what I'm saying, though there's stuff in there about Dad, her new family, and the one I'll have some day, which she'll never know about because I wont be calling her anymore.

I slam down the phone, and I'm back in my body again, crying and gasping for breath like a little kid who just got whipped. I scan the tidy trailer. It feels like a bomb has gone off, and I'm ready to make a run for it when Mr.

Deere walks over and puts his hand on my shoulder. "It's alright," he says, and looks at me like I'm a human being again. He leaves his wife with Brad, and leads me into the back yard to catch my breath. In the morning he takes us home, and in a matter of weeks the last vestiges of my old life fall away.

15

THE BOYS OF SUMMER

Last summer, while Mom was marrying Ray in Galveston, my friend Bill killed three people in the grocery store by our house. I'd known him since I was thirteen, and we had gone to see Van Halen together the last time they were in town. I thought about Bill the whole way back from White Deer. Realistically, it didn't seem like I was headed toward committing murder, but there were parallels in our lives that were frightening me.

Bill was older than us, and we all looked up to him. When we dreamed about being able to drive, for instance, we always imagined ourselves like Bill, shirtless and barefoot, with one arm out the window, and a cigarette in the steering wheel hand. He even had a cool backstory. After getting into trouble with drugs and alcohol, Bill met Joey's big sister, Mandy. He cleaned up, they started dating, and he got a job at the IGA where he worked his way up to assistant manager. He seemed totally mellow, but every once in a while he'd tell you about someone he'd just beaten up outside of a 7-11. These were strange conversations, but not because of what he was saying; it was more his emotional distance from it. I wasn't afraid of him though. Nor did I want him to stop telling me "I beat someone up," stories. To the contrary, he had tracked down some bullies for me once, and I was happy to have a tough guy in my corner.

Bill and Mandy broke up when she caught him using drugs again. Then the grocery store fired him and he vanished. He must have gone back to the old crowd, because a year later he stuck up the IGA on the graveyard shift.

A triple murder will make the news almost anywhere, but in Edmond, Oklahoma it is earth shaking; and for some reason, I knew it was Bill as soon as I heard about it. Within twenty-four hours the police had him. He had bragged to his friends about breaking a gunstock on the skull of one of the men he killed. Then he took the $1,400 dollars he stole, threw an afternoon party, and went on a shopping spree.

For months after his arrest, Bill was paraded across the television in an orange jumpsuit, as the District Attorney gave press conference after press conference promising to deliver the death penalty. It was surreal, and one day I was downtown and ran into Mandy coming out of the courthouse. She was crying so hard she couldn't talk. Her dad was holding her, and I found out later that she was there as a character witness during the sentencing portion of the trial. They were probably hoping she could humanize him, but all it really did was break her heart, because from the instant Bill decided to rob the IGA, he was headed straight for death row.

There may have always been something dead inside of Bill. I'm not sure. For a long time I walled it off and tried not to think about it. But I was aware then, and I am more aware now, that decision-making was at the heart of the trouble he caused for himself, his family, and his victims. And even if he didn't have a conscience, simple intuition must have given him some kind of warning along the way. Life is like that. Sometimes when it's trying to tell you something, you get a little nudge here or a hazy sign there, and other times, it just kicks in the door and shoves a boot up your ass.

By the time we broke down in Amarillo, I could've opened a Western store with all the boots I'd collected. I wasn't even a senior in high school yet, and I'd already been arrested six times, and for really dumb stuff. I got drunk in a bar when I was in the eighth grade and shoplifted a bottle of beer. My mom and grandpa had to come pick me up at the jailhouse. I remember staggering side to side out of the booking hall while they walked behind me. Not a proud moment.

Another time, my buddies and I were aiming a toy gun at people in traffic; which was already foolish, but my friend was trying to sell his car, and his name and phone number were in the windshield in big block letters. And one night, we stole a bunch of blinking lights off of some hazard signs and kept them in my trunk – which flashed like a beacon until the cops found them. I even got arrested in the police station once while trying to help a friend who got pulled over for D.U.I.

I obviously wasn't going to have to kill anyone to get the attention of the law, but on the other hand, I was definitely running out of second chances.

We got back from White Deer, Texas on a Monday afternoon and found an eviction notice on our door. We caught our breath and called Wal-Mart, and they fired us for not showing up for our last two shifts. A few hours later, I was uptown and got approached by a football player who wanted to buy a bag of pot. I'd made the mistake of getting high with him once, and he stopped by our house every week for the rest of the summer looking for weed. He was a world class dickhead, so I never once gave him so much as a seed or a stem, and because of my recent experiences in Texas, and recurring thoughts of Bill, I wanted desperately not to be the guy that people thought of when they were looking to score drugs. So I asked this guy to please not come over for marijuana anymore, and he beat the shit out of me in front of about fifteen people.

That pretty much sealed it. Edmond was cordially inviting me to fuck off, so we wrecked the house and moved out the next day; and that was the last I saw of Brad. Me and Abear, the world's most loyal dog, house-hopped for a couple weeks, and then we lived on Tommy's couch for about three more. His roommate, a six foot seven inch Felix Unger, wanted us gone the minute we got there, so when Mom called with a message from Dad, I was all ears. He was willing to pay for the car repairs if I drove straight from Groom to Phoenix and did my senior year of high school out there. Mom may have hated this idea even more than I did, but we lacked a viable alternative plan, so it was agreed. And after two more weeks of the same old shit, I was back on the road to Groom with Tommy and Blossom, the ugliest kid at the golf course.

16

I-40

Groom, Texas must be the hottest place on the planet. Or maybe it just feels that way because I am always hung-over and exposed to the elements when I visit. Last night, me and Tommy met a couple of girls in back of a diner in White Deer. I told them I played guitar for Brian Adams, and we had sex with them at the motor lodge while Blossom sat on the floor and talked to their sister. For awhile, my girl and I were doing it in the tub while the shower ran, and now I have a giant friction burn on my dick. It's more annoying than painful, but I can't quit looking at it and contemplating the many infections which this may have opened me up to. I tried to ask her sister if there was anything I should be on the look out for, venereal disease-wise, and she went straight inside and told on me. Then they left in a huff.

Now I'm lying on a sticky vinyl bench in a broken down school bus in back of Mr. Bivens' garage, waiting for him to finish my car. I could have sworn he said it was done when

I called, but what good would arguing do? Besides, he and Mrs. Bivens have invited me over for lunch this afternoon, and that kind of hospitality doesn't grow on trees. In the meantime, though, I am suffering my usual morning-after attack of thought. Which almost always wraps around to Andie.

She's back in Edmond now. Her family returned just as abruptly as they moved away, and because I had no right to pry, I accepted the reason she gave me and just enjoyed the chance to talk with her while the whole world wasn't whirling apart. She stopped by Tommy's apartment the day before I left and it was like seeing a ghost; except the ghost was me. My life in Oklahoma was over, and after all the noise I'd made, she was the one who was going to stay. She also clearly wasn't pregnant anymore, so the dream of our family, however unrealistic it may have been, was gone as well. This just couldn't be anything other than what it was; good-bye forever to each other, and to the last whisper of innocence.

We wound up in bed almost immediately, and for an instant we were back under her blanket in the house on the hill, floating up to that cloud where only we existed. Then, before anything even happened, it just stopped, and we were waking up in an x-ray machine. Whatever we had was gone, and like middle school, and high school, and childhood itself, it wasn't coming back. We looked into each other's eyes long enough to see tears, and then Andie was gone too.

When Tommy and Blossom left Groom this morning they took my last real connection to Oklahoma with them. I still have some distant and aging relatives there, but to be honest, I've been gone less than a day and I can't think of anyone who would want me to return. I miss it terribly, and I don't want to leave, but an inventory of my possessions tells the story of why I must: I have Abear, a hangover, a grocery bag full of dirty clothes, seventeen dollars and change, a broken heart, and a scab on my penis. Not exactly a ringing endorsement for anything I have done on my own behalf, or anyone else's.

Going to Phoenix is surrender. Not in a practical sense, because I know Mom won't want to monitor where I go or what I do, but showing up under these conditions is emotional forfeit. She and Ray will have superiority and the "I told you so," factor, and I will own whatever the opposite of that is. There is Emily, my baby sister, and I really do love her. But aside from the time I'll have with her, there is exactly nothing to look forward to.

Still, I know I couldn't have gone on living like I was. Eventually I would have wrecked a car, or my petty crimes would have grown into felonies. The drinking definitely would have put a barrier around my prospects for the future, and I probably would have achieved my goal of impregnating some poor girl who would have been stuck with me the way I, in turn, would have been chained to the Wal-Mart, or some other dead end job.

But who cares about that now. I have my car back, and Mr. and Mrs. Bivens have bid me farewell. The sun is setting in the desert, and I've covered about half of the three hundred and thirty miles between Groom and the Albuquerque Airport, where I'll pick up Ray and drive four hundred and twenty more to Phoenix. The crying started as I crossed out of Amarillo, and hasn't really stopped since. I am exhausted in every conceivable way, and there is something about a shitload of cactuses and a whole bunch of nothing that really drives a lonely point home.

Ray is waiting at the curb when I arrive at the airport in New Mexico. He isn't always an asshole, just most of the time, and tonight I am happy to see him. He is just twenty-five, but he's as close to a parent as anyone I've been around in awhile, and I am willing, after the summer I've had and the drive I've just made, to take some comfort in that. He has no bags, so I get out and hand him the keys. Then I curl up in the floorboard, lay my head in the passenger seat, and instantly fall into a deep and dreamless sleep.

PART TWO

PHOENIX

(With a Brief Return to Oklahoma)

1

PHOENIX

Tonight I am graduating from high school. This is a minor miracle, and to pull it off I had to take a full load of classes, attend night school, and do correspondence courses. I have never been so bored, but it feels like I'm accomplishing something, though that may just be pacifying my mother.

When I got here almost a year ago, I wanted to change my life, but I wasn't sure how. I spent the first month or two crying, and the next few hanging out with the cocaine, beer, and mushrooms crowd, but gradually academics and a job working in the locker room of a racquet club squeezed out the time I normally would have used to cause trouble. I've also been sinking myself into the one good habit I brought with me from Oklahoma – bodybuilding. Most nights I spend at the gym, and it seems to be paying off. I'm bigger now, more confident, and exercising eases the depression, which I thought was the result of the hangovers I'd subjected myself to from about twelve years old on, but seems now to be a regular part of my life. So I guess I'm doing better, but I can't figure out what it's all adding up to, or where am I heading.

It's strange to be back in Phoenix. I kind of liked it when I was little; but now, not so much. We live in Tempe, way across town socially and geographically from our old house near Camelback Mountain, but still in the same metropolitan area. It's not an easy place to describe, but if Edmond is Pony Boy from "The Outsiders," then Phoenix is the Tidy Bowl Man, cheerfully motoring around a hyper-chlorinated and rapidly evaporating backyard swimming pool.

The city trumpets its cowboys-and-Indians past, but today it is a sprawling grid of wide streets, stucco ranch houses, and strip malls, great and small. The better neighborhoods have murky manmade lakes, and the best ones have golf courses irrigated with smelly canal water. I've met a few native Arizonans, but it seems like most of the people here are transplants from places like Wisconsin - where it is cold and there is even less to do - working for one of the massive corporations headquartered around town.

Of course, the main thing about Phoenix is the heat. For six months out of the year it feels like you're living in a blast furnace. Bath towels dry before they hit the ground and cars turn into saunas when you leave them. In the summer, big dead grass parks stand empty because the sand and monkey bars burn your feet and hands; and almost all non-essential outdoor activity ceases. There are those who love the natural beauty of the desert – like retirees, javelinas, and the chupacabre - but to me it is a scorching, sterile, existential void, and I want out, bad.

The only problem is college. I feel like I ought to go, and Arizona State is right down the road. They have accepted me, as they do anyone who can fog a mirror, and I guess that's where I'm headed.

Tonight, however, I will walk into a tiny stadium full of people I don't know, wearing a graduation gown made of Halloween costume material, and pick up my high school diploma. I am sincerely proud of this achievement, but Ray is the really big winner because now he can eyeball me even harder to get the hell out already.

Phoenix isn't all bad, though. Eventually it cools off, and there are some decent people here. The dog track is fun and I like the football stadium, mostly because I saw The Rolling Stones there in the seventh grade. I also have good memories of Veterans Memorial Coliseum and Compton Terrace, where I first discovered the explosive wonderland of live music. This is actually one of the things that keep going through my mind. Like maybe there is something for me to do in concerts that pays more than ten imaginary dollars a night.

I'm eighteen now, so I can legally work at bars, and I could probably swing a job at one of the clubs by the college through my friends at the gym. That would be fun, and sort of interesting. But as you drive out of Tempe, north toward the mountain, and the idealism and excitement of college life drifts away, you notice an inordinate number of strip clubs, which all appear to have been around for about twenty years. I'm really drawn to those places, and not just for the obvious reasons. Yes, I love girls. And naked girls, so much the better. But I swear I can feel the heartbreak and anger and frustration and sex reaching out to me through those windowless walls. It's like I'm ten years old again, and that fucking Squeeze Box is daring me to learn a little more. I haven't set foot in a strip club since Florida, but I am curious, and also confident that I am still young enough to indulge my interest without getting any permanent scars. There is something for me there, and I feel sometimes like Denzel in the Malcolm X movie, where the camera holds him in frame as he floats toward a destination larger than his own intentions.

But for now, I'll shut it out. Whatever that draw to the dark side is, it's probably better left unexplored. College is an unequal but opposite force, and if I can shift my interests in that direction maybe I can develop a strong, focused, all-purpose, productive will like Arnold. I don't want to be a loser anymore. I want to succeed. I want to rise above all the nonsense I've come from and created, and be a decent person. I want to find a girl and be her hero. I want to have my own family, and deserve it, and I want to walk in the light and be a good example. I just want things to turn out well, so college - definitely college. That's the way to go.

2

THE NEW CAREER

In the summer after high school, I started working at a college bar called After The Gold Rush.. It was a cavernous place that had peaked a generation earlier, and was keeping the doors open with concerts and dangerously overcrowded teen nights. The décor was Matterhorn meets Saturday Night Fever, and their signature attraction was a sad laser light show peppered with limp ejaculations of stage fog, which was performed by a DJ who lived to put it on. This was a holdover from the club's late seventies heyday, and people generally seemed confused when it started, as it wore on, and when it finished. I dreaded this spectacle because the coda to the swirling lights finale was an announcement to the ladies in the house that the doormen were available to dance with anyone who asked. We were already wearing pink tux shirts with matching bow ties and cummerbunds, and trying to project authority while navigating the many movements of Whitesnake's "Still of the Night" was way beyond my limitations as a dancer.

This, and the girls who pressed us into service were almost all doing it to make their friends laugh.

Still, I was eighteen, and for the first few weeks I couldn't believe I was getting paid to stand around in a bar and act cool. I did some exploring and found a good hiding place for the taxi-dance announcement, and when I was eventually discovered, I received a welcome demotion to parking lot security, where my job was sitting on the tailgate of my Blazer with a pitcher of Diet Coke, reading muscle magazines and talking to girls. This also allowed me to trade in my quasi-tux for a polo shirt and jeans, which was incredibly liberating.

It was in the Gold Rush's sprawling, weed filled lot that I met the first exotic dancer I ever made sweet love to. Her name was Crystal, and she had a kind of Goth flapper look, which didn't really match her laid back personality. We talked for an hour or so, and when I clocked out, she came to my mom's house to go swimming.

We got to Mom's at about two in the morning. I stripped down to my boxers and swam a lap, then we tip-toed back to my room and had sex. There wasn't anything crazy about it, nor was any larger lesson learned about strippers in general. We were both teenagers, still living at home - and in the same neighborhood, no less - so our professional roles (such as they were) were basically trumped.

When I dropped Crystal off, she told me a joke as she got out of the car. We laughed, and that was pretty much that. If we had met six months earlier, we might have been high school sweethearts. But probably not.

I met Dylan, my instant best friend, at the Gold Rush too, and we bonded over bodybuilding. He was the head bouncer, which meant he got to wear a turtleneck and card people in the lobby. He was by far the biggest guy on staff, and probably the best looking too, but his Achilles heels were laziness and entitlement. He would come outside, while on the clock, and sleep in my truck for up to an hour at a time; and I was amazed at his indignance when he got fired for it. He yelled, and threatened the manager of the club - a thirty-ish man who walked with a cane – when he didn't even have a position to defend. It was just, "Fuck you, Clayton, where in the hell do you get off, you gimpy asshole!"

At the end of his tirade, Dylan wanted me to quit in solidarity, but I just couldn't make myself walk out on a perfectly good job over someone else's right to nap on company time. However, my hours were cut due to complicity in his crimes, and I needed money to get out of Mom's place, where the living situation was tense and getting worse. She was not happy to see me when I arrived from Oklahoma a year earlier, and to Ray, I was basically a houseguest who wouldn't leave. They had just moved again – this time to Mesa - and Ray shared his displeasure with my continued presence in his home by punching a half a dozen holes in the walls after I took a t-shirt from his drawer without asking. It was pretty clearly time to giddy-up, the only problem was where to.

After much worrying, the answer came to me during an evening of heavy metal under the stars.

At an Iron Maiden show at Compton Terrace, I met two strippers in civilian clothes. They were pretty-ish, but hard, and almost as soon as we started talking, one of them asked me if I wanted to fuck in the bushes. That sounded like something to take a rain check on because she was a) clearly longer in the tooth than the twenty-five years she was claiming, and b) probably some biker's old lady. They were, however, cool people, and once we'd written off the sex, I got the lowdown on their place of business.

Bourbon Street Circus was a Phoenix institution, and I had definitely heard of it. These girls worked the day shift – which I later learned was where old dancers go to die – and when I told them I needed work, they promised to put in the good word.

I went to Bourbon Street the next morning, bright and early. They had just opened and already the parking lot was half full. No rest for the horny, I guessed, but from the outside it looked like the last place you'd go looking for fun – or women. The building had faded red trim, and a sign with painted ivy meant to imply New Orleans, but for the most part it was just an old white box on a square slab of black top.

I parked, and as I approached the heavy steel door, I thought how ridiculous it seemed to iron a shirt and comb your hair to visit a center of sleaze before noon on a weekday. And because I am always reaching for the most dramatic way to explain things to myself, it also crossed my mind that I was fulfilling a prophecy which was revealed to me two and a half years prior during a wild night in Florida with a couple of gay men.

When I entered the narrow hall leading into the club, the abrupt shift from light to darkness struck me blind for about ten seconds. It was scary because I still wasn't sure if

I was allowed to be there. I'd heard you only had to be eighteen to work at a topless bar, but getting thrown out before my eyes adjusted seemed like a real possibility. This was so different from my only other experience with nudie bars, and it actually reminded me more of a carnival sideshow I went to at the state fair when I was nine years old. The barker was offering a look at an "E.T. Smurf" for a dollar, which sounded pretty cool until I went behind the curtain and saw a dwarf, horribly deformed by Thalidomide, wearing a white elf's hat. I'll never forget him, and I was getting the same sense of dread from the commotion around the corner - but it was too late to turn back now.

Up ahead, I heard J. Geils' cover of *Land of a Thousand Dances* and a D.J. boosting two for one drafts in a coked up game show host's voice. There was cigarette smoke, cheap perfume, and the vinegar stench of rotten liquor coming from the rubber mats behind the bar.

At the end of the hall I got my sight back, and I was surprised to find a big room that was two-thirds blacked out. A boozy cast of characters was watching a topless woman dance on a corner stage, but it wasn't busy enough yet to open the whole place. The crowd reminded me of the *People In Your Neighborhood* song from Sesame Street. Even at this hour, all walks of life were represented, joined together to stare like hungry wolves at a revolving crew of ladies of the morning.

My objective was the opposite of theirs. I didn't want to seem like an amateur, so I needed to not stare, which was difficult because I was stranded at the stanchion roping off the entrance for what felt like a month, but was probably closer to a minute. At last, I saw one of the girls from the night before. I waved at her like a long lost relative, and she waved back, then signaled a tall, pale guy in a dark suit coat. As they talked, I did a quick scan of the rest of the room and clocked five stages, two bars, black walls, black ceiling, brass poles, charcoal mirrors, and a lot of old metal chairs with red vinyl seat cushions. As seedy bars go, it was pretty ordinary, but a strong vibe of decadence and the sight of nearly naked women in public made my stomach drop like a roller coaster.

The next five minutes went by pretty fast. The guy with the glasses turned out to be Phil, the head doorman. We talked a little, and I liked his quick wit and readiness to be sarcastic about anything. The girl from the concert sat with me while I filled out my job application, though she didn't say much, and when I was done Phil hired me. The deal was simple. The shifts were eight hours and you had to wear a black coat and tie. There was no eating on the clock or fucking the dancers. Joe Mack was the big boss, and he traveled between this club and a few others around the Valley and in Tucson. If he liked you, you could stay. If he didn't, you were gone.

The only other thing that struck me as I left was the complete lack of pretense in the crowd. I had only been out of high school for a few months and I was used to adults switching on their grown-up face when I entered a room. There were no such allowances for youth in this place. I saw girls who couldn't have been any older than me, and no one seemed surprised that we were there, or ready to alter their behavior because of it. Conversely, The Gold Rush was a college bar, a dying one, but a college bar nonetheless. On most nights it could still feel exuberant, and an air of self-discovery drifted over from the university. Bourbon Street had none of that; at least not in an enriching way. It was a real life, honest-to-goodness shithole, and even during a fairly sedate day shift it vibrated with darkness and sex and consequence. There would be no punches pulled in here, and as I looked back I couldn't help thinking, "If Mom could see me now."

3

APRIL

When I arrived in Arizona for my senior year of high school, I felt like damaged goods. So much freedom had already come my way that I honestly didn't know how to relate to regular kids anymore. I'd been living like a little Nero for years, with no one telling me what to do or where to go. I was free to drink and smoke dope and have sex whenever I wanted, and if my friends and I got bored, we jumped in the car and went out looking for trouble. We stole, we vandalized, we fought, and we did these things at any hour of the day or night we pleased. Since the fifth grade it had been this way. I was sneaking around then, but by the time I was a freshman, my mother was barely even pretending to care what I did, and she was gone half the week anyway. So when she left Oklahoma, and I got my own place, well, that just made it all official.

Phoenix was a whole different world from Edmond. It was much bigger, more impersonal, and there wasn't a strong parochial community to rebel against. Most of the people in our area were from other places, so they didn't really keep track of each other; and the religious influence, which is everywhere in Oklahoma, was almost non-existent. In Edmond, the Baptists wouldn't let you wear shorts to the gym, let alone school, and on my first day of classes in Tempe, I was shocked to see girls with tattoos and tank tops, and guys in cut offs and flip flops. These things just did not fly in the Sooner State, and the hazy boundaries of the Phoenix suburbs made it difficult to establish my identity relative to the town and the other kids.

Then there was the issue of being a "kid" in the first place. I was seventeen, but I felt thirty-five, and the more time I had to think about the things I'd done back in Edmond, the more shame I felt. In one of the rare conversations I had with my father during this period, he yelled and said I'd ruined Andie's life. That really sunk in, and definitely felt true. Then, shortly before I left town, I got picked up doing a gasoline drive off with a couple of girls. The cop who arrested us knew me, and he said something like, "These kids follow you around and all you ever do is make trouble for them." Then he looked me in the eye and said, "You are a user."

But it was more than just these two brief conversations that had me thinking. I knew where I'd been and what I'd done, and I didn't trust myself anymore, especially around girls. I loved Andie more than I ever thought I could love anything, and I'd blown up both of our lives; and, of course, negatively influenced almost everyone who ever spent any kind of time with me. And so, when I got to Arizona, I froze.

For a while I tried to do the stuff I used to do, but it just made me seem crazy. I'd get hammered and rip off a twelve pack from a convenience store, and if there were three guys along for the ride, one of them would look at me like I was an outlaw, and the other two would split and never talk to me again. Or I'd hide away from females until I wound up drunk at a party and had to be pulled off of one. A few girls from school came around anyway, but I got the feeling they were looking for a nice, normal boy from a regular family, and that just wasn't me. I really wanted it to be, but inevitably I'd tell the wrong story about my former life and kids would either think I was a liar, a nutcase, or a show-off, liar, nutcase.

In the end, I decided to keep it all secret. I didn't bring anyone to the house to meet Mom and Ray, and I tried to say as little as possible about where I'd come from or what I'd been up to. This helped to avoid uncomfortable situations, but it also drove me back into loner mode because people – especially girl people - know when you're uneasy with yourself, and they avoid it like the plague.

School was worst of all, and I felt like an imposter every time I walked on campus. It was such a happy, sterile place, full of cheerful retarded innocence. No one was pregnant or drunk or openly racist, and all the chattering about ball games, family vacations, and college made me feel simultaneously conspicuous and invisible. My classmates seemed so comfortable with each other. And when they gathered at the senior assembly to celebrate their culminating years of togetherness, the "Most Likely To" awards spawned roars of knowing giggles that flew past me like winged photo albums of people I'd never met.

I felt like I was showing up at a wedding right after the bride left. And nowhere did I feel dirtier and out of place than typing class, where I was forced to sit in the warm, angelic glow of April Trueheart; a virtuous beam of untouchable purity with auburn hair, beatific eyes, and a smile that sung, "The world abounds with infinite love – and you may not have sex with me."

April was the obvious favorite of our be-Dockered, mustachioed instructor, who allowed himself two joking interactions and one fond good-bye with her per day. He was a nice enough man, but for a while I suspected he was a sadist when he parked me right next to her, in the row directly in front of his desk. It was torture. I could literally feel the heat from her body, but even the slightest conversation tied my tongue. Plus, we always had an adult audience, so even if I could get a brief exchange going, nerves and self-consciousness would end it before it got anywhere.

And that's how it stayed, all semester long, as I typed and suffered, and suffered and typed, doing penance for my sins, and privately wondering why, oh why, I had eaten the apple of wisdom when heaven might have been within my reach.

4

HAPPY HOUR

When I told my mother I was going to work at a topless bar, she warned me not to marry any of the girls there – and she wasn't kidding. I was eighteen, and not even dating anyone, so her caution felt like a complete non-sequitur. Still, it had the ring of truth, and though I laughed it off, I felt like maybe she could see something I couldn't.

It seemed ridiculous, though, to say such a thing when life was finally going good again. I was in my first semester of college, and while I was secretly burned out after augmenting a full load of high school classes with correspondence and night courses in order to graduate on time, Mom didn't know that. I was bigger and stronger too, the result of increased hours in the gym and a headlong dive into steroids. I had even resigned myself to living in Arizona, this after a failed return to Oklahoma – where I pulled into Edmond, picked up where I left off, enraged Tommy's roommate, took a gang beating at a teen night club, and drove back through the desert with my tail between my legs, all in about three weeks.

The corner had clearly been turned, and if Mom couldn't see that, well, that was her problem. So what if I had just been fired from an auto dealership for sideswiping a Taurus with a stakebed truck? And, okay, so I left a house-framing job after three days with a broken toe which may or may not have been broken. And fine, the front desk position at the gym hadn't worked out, and the Gold Rush was sort of drifting away, and my employment during senior year – janitor, locker room attendant, Kmart shelf stocker, and construction site clean up crew member – had followed the same general pattern. That was ancient history, and the sky was clear now. My will was strong, my nightclub bouncing skills were on the rise, and my ambitions were through the roof. I was going to get a business degree, enroll in an M.B.A./J.D. program, conquer Hollywood, then withdraw from society to live in the forest with my wife and children (whom I would, again, be finding somewhere outside of a topless bar).

So, I totally didn't get Mom's concern; but, you know, I didn't get anything about her, really.

I went back to Bourbon Street on a Thursday during happy hour for my first night of work, and found a totally different scene than the one I'd encountered a few mornings prior. The lot was packed, and people were walking over from across the street and around the corner. I was wearing a whole lot of black - pants, Reeboks, Goodwill jacket, and clip-on tie (which would pull away in a struggle) - over a white shirt and socks, when I encountered Phil and a crew of four big and tall guys who were all dressed like me. It was getting close to sundown, and they were having a quick smoke before the night officially got underway. I shook hands with everyone, then Phil told me to go inside and start walking the floor. If I saw empty beer glasses I was supposed to pick them up, and if the guys were touching the girls, I was to extend a warning. This sounded pretty straight forward, except that no one knew me; and wouldn't they be confused by a strange guy pacing around the bar picking stuff up and giving orders? "Absolutely not," Phil replied, and as I entered the room I saw why.

5

SWEET DREAMS

The air is thick with smoke, and crackling with dirty, black electricity. It's dark, purple neon sizzles, music booms, and I, in a bad suit, am speed walking with arms full of sloshing beer glasses through a frenzied mob of yellow-toothed men and gyrating naked women, who laugh maniacally as I pass, and reach for me like a swarm of horny zombies. It's terrifying, but the pornographic pull of this place is overpowering. Some unholy corner of my mind has taken over. I know I should leave, but instead I'm racing around the narrow track – the only clear path available - as though there was some way to get out of this madness without sprinting for the door.

I'm exhausted, and my eyelids are dropping like anvils. I can barely stagger now, so I climb under a bench in the back of the club, hoping that no one will catch me pilfering a few seconds of sleep. But they always do, and I wake up in the same howling, naked, Bon Jovi blasting chaos - only now the regional overlord, Joe Mack, is standing over me, glaring.

Sweating and panicked, I open my eyes in a new room, ready to jump back on the floor and gather up more empties. I can't make sense of this yet, but I'll run faster, I'll seat more dirtheads, I'll swat more hands off of more exposed legs, and I'll keep on running, always running, like the Devil himself is chasing me.

"I'm sorry!" I scream out to no one. "Please..."

A few seconds pass, then I realize I'm sitting on a mattress on the floor at Mom's house. No one is chasing me, and Joe Mack is wherever Joe Mack goes when he's not in some Godforsaken titty bar in the middle of the desert. I'm just having another nightmare; but good fucking luck getting back to sleep.

***

It goes on this way for weeks as I slowly acclimate to my new environment. It's just nothing at all like that first, relatively boring morning. If anything, it feels more like super charged high school with public nudity and rowdy, leering men. This time, however, I am not a black sheep. To the total contrary, I'm one of the normal ones; and, dare I say, the stable ones. I don't ramble on about my past anymore, but I can tell from talking to the girls here that if I did, no one would bat an eyelash. There is a commonality that I haven't felt since Brad and I lived together. And even then, we were an oddity, far outnumbered by the regular people in town. Now, I feel – well, normal, and at home.

At least half of the dancers, like me, are not old enough to be here as customers. Our bodies have gotten us in the door early. The girls are developed, and I am big and strong, but I certainly don't feel like an adult yet, and I'll bet it's the same for them. I imagine us as a tribe of dirty kids who have seen too much too soon, and I am their protector, making sure nothing too horrible happens during our communal hallucination.

The older ones — that is, everyone over twenty-one — do not count. Resignation is slowing their electrons, and hardening them into something sad and permanent. We, on the other hand, are young. We could still rocket out of here and never look back because we are just visiting. We could still be happy, and married, and rich, and famous, and make peace with our families, and be parents, and own comfortable homes with big green lawns and silly dogs. We could have careers and degrees and be doctors or models or lawyers or actors or rock stars' wives. And that's because for us, this topless bar is temporary, like an extended one-night stand. We are just kids who have stumbled into the grown-ups' party, and we are proud to be in on the joke.

Still, most of us wouldn't have come this way if things had been different. It's like one day you are little and there is too much of this and not enough of that. You are alone for a long time, and then you are here, with an understanding in your eyes, almost like a secret handshake. No one articulates anything, but when the frat boys arrive by the drunken busload, with their roaring sense of naïve entitlement, we understand that we are not them. We won't go proudly home for Christmas, or walk the red carpet into the establishment, because we are on the sordid side of things; even if they are the ones who got shitfaced and drove across town to ogle girls.

It's awkward, but such is life, and when you've run away from that, or been excluded from it, you understand that it wouldn't fit you anyway. It's like trying to believe in Santa Claus again. Not possible, and in the end, not productive.

There is one obvious caveat to this quasi-camaraderie, though. Guys cannot be full members of the tribe because we are not making ourselves vulnerable in the same ways. We are not getting naked, or violating any heavy taboo. We are not standing on a stage risking rejection, or daring our families to shun us; and if we quit in a year or so, the stigma won't follow us like it will them. There is also no wolf pack of the opposite sex lining up outside to moon over us, or offer real money for a few minutes of our time. The sad fact of the matter is, the females are the stars, and we, the lowly and terrifically common males, are invisible. Which, of course, means our income is a tiny fraction of theirs because no one ever went to a nudie bar to check out the bouncers.

I wonder how they do it, though. I mean, where in the world does a young girl get the nerve to walk into a place like this, take off all her clothes, and serve herself up to a bunch of wild-eyed crazy people, many of whom are old enough to be her father or grandpa? It must be scary as hell. I've been trying to learn about where they come from, and it seems like most dancers' families do not know, at least initially, what they're up to. Probably a lot of them aren't close enough to care. A few have "cool" moms, but for the most part, strippers, especially young ones, are out on an island.

Things move fast in here, and I've already watched a wave of new girls break off into little sisterhoods. They declare themselves best friends, go everywhere together, and often become roommates, but their facades seem to have the primary relationship. It's strange. No one wants to identify too closely with this life, but no one wants to be alone either. So they go by their stage names, even when they are away from the club. I couldn't say why, exactly, but most other kinds of privacy fall away when they walk in the door, and withholding given names and actual selves may be a way to compensate. They might also be protecting their futures or denying the present. Who knows. It's real, though, and pressing too hard for a dancer's actual first name is like pushing a civilian girl to show you her tits. Bad form, really bad form.

But before I paint myself as a pure protective big brother, let me confess that I may be more turned on by all of this than the most depraved, degenerate dirtbag. Spending an unguarded minute talking to a girl you've already seen naked throws an intimacy switch in your brain that is completely artificial, but totally exhilarating. And I get the atom bomb version of that when Joe Mack sends me into the dressing room to collect shift fees (the seven dollars a night dancers pay to work here). The dimensions are about the same as the master bedroom in a tract home, and it is completely full of undressed women. Sometimes they stop their primping to chat or tease, and I try to be casual, but it's usually everything I can do to keep a straight face. Often they're not wearing anything at all, which is fantastic, and the stuff they do to get ready amazes me. Topless dancing is technically illegal in Phoenix, so before they hit the floor the girls twist their nipples to make them stand up, then cover them with the flesh colored part of a band-aid. I guess this makes them legally clothed, but to my way of thinking this process is underscoring the nudity, not softening it up for public consumption. Whose job is it to dream up these ridiculous boundaries anyway? Probably some little man in an ugly government office who would be so much happier if he would let go of his dick, and come to work here, because watching this, and the million other grooming rituals these girls unabashedly perform right in front of you, is the very best kind of overwhelming.

And it doesn't stop there. The dancing part of the dancer probably says more about who they are than anything short of an unguarded conversation, and some of these girls can really move. It probably also goes without saying that most of them are fun to look at. I've been trying to perfect my aloof and unaffected stare into the middle distance, but like all of the other weirdoes in here, I wait for their tops to come off, even though they just did one song ago. I have no alibi. I am a gross, grunting monkey, and I flat out love this place. It is a big, sexy tragedy full of gorgeous birds with broken wings, and it sings to me like the Sirens of Ulysses, or the first time I heard The Beatles. Fuck, sometimes it's like being drunk and stoned and frying on acid all at once. Better, actually. Take that feeling of intoxication, wrap it in the little boy thrill of finding a stash of porno magazines, then pour the Muppet Movie joy of putting on a show on top of it all, and you're almost there. It's like, DAMN! You know what I mean?

I have, however, done enough drugs to know that this kind of high always comes with a crash, and one hell of a hangover. When you lose your common sense and let your id run wild, incredibly bad things can happen. And if I was feeling dead to normal girls before, then now what? Maybe Mom was right. Maybe I do need to be careful not to get married in a place like this. Maybe I ought to do something to protect myself from all of these aggressive, uninhibited girls with their harrowing back stories (and front stories) and perfect asses. Arggghhhh!

I feel like God is trying to tell me something; to warn me before I go too far. I get a shiver down my spine every time I pass that timekeeper who works behind the bar. It may just be that she looks exactly like April, the beautiful angel virgin from typing class, who tormented me with her unapproachable goodness. That almost has to be it, really. This is totally the kind of stuff God pulls. Never too on the nose, always with the symbolism and fleeting metaphor. Just once, though, it would be nice to hear him say something directly. But I guess that would be too...

Hey, wait a minute. That is April from typing class.

6

AT PLAY IN THE FIELDS OF THE LORD

I was ten years old the first time I kissed a girl. It was all set up by phone. She had three of her friends over to witness the event, and Matt and Mike were standing by to be my seconds. All I had to do was ride six miles on my bike, around the mountain, to her garage, then beat back the butterflies, pucker up, and perform. I did it too, before an audience of stunned fifth graders, who, in an ensuing moment of awed silence, stared at me like I was their king. Then everyone giggled, and my buddies and I rode home on flying bicycles just like the boys in E.T. – or at least that's how it felt.

When I was eleven, I kissed lots of girls, and turned down my first bona fide offer of intercourse from Cindy, a fast eighth grader with a retarded little brother. We were alone in my room and she was letting me touch her boobs. I was astonished by the way they felt, and could have gone on squeezing until my mom came home; but when she asked me if I wanted to make love, I froze. I wasn't entirely sure what she meant. The basics of human reproduction were clear enough, but "make love" sounded like it might be a poetic euphemism for a more formal kind of making out or romantic affection. The whole issue scared me to death, and "No!" jumped out of my mouth before I had a chance to think about it. And I was already contemplating a backpedal when she walked out the door, got on her bicycle and rode away.

Then Oklahoma happened. We were there visiting when I was twelve, and another boy and I were taking turns kissing an older girl in the tall grass. It was like spin the bottle without the bottle, until I put my hand down her pants. This changed the tone abruptly, and my friend got scared and ran off. I didn't know what to do. I'd gotten so carried away with the groping, I sort of forgot myself, and now that we were alone I felt an obligation to follow through; so I went down on her - sort of. The mechanics of this act were years beyond me, so I basically copied what I'd seen the cows doing with their salt licks. This went on for a minute or two, and when it was over I was completely freaked out. The whole situation down there was just not what I was expecting at all, and it made me think that we were definitely doing something very, very wrong.

I walked back to my grandparents' apartment and waited for the cops to come and arrest me. There was a comfortable place at the end of the couch, and I decided to spend my last hours of freedom there, with my family, who were completely oblivious to the disgrace I had brought upon us all. A rerun of M.A.S.H. was on, and my eyes darted from Mom, to my grandparents, to my aunts, and back again, until I gradually relaxed enough to watch with them. "What the hell," I thought, "Let them enjoy these last few minutes of peace before the sky falls." But the sky didn't fall. And though my heart was pounding in my throat, I drew strength from Hawkeye Pierce, the world's most lovable pervert, and resisted the compulsion to confess. And thank God, because the police never came.

I was thirteen when I closed the deal. It was right after my banishment to Edmond, and I was riding the school bus to my friend Neil's, when Debbie, a seventh grader I had never met before, asked me over to her house.

It was weird from the get-go because right after we got there she was inviting us to warm our hands on her breasts. An extremely gracious gesture which was undercut by the presence of her slightly older brother, who was lurking around the periphery, trying not to seem too interested.

Five minutes later, Debbie and I were in her bedroom making out, and the pace went from pogo stick to rocket ship in the blink of an eye. Her shirt was up, her underwear came off, and suddenly, it was decision time. I thought about turning back, but she said she had done it before, and my friend was waiting outside. Leaving would have been extremely lame, plus I really wanted this to happen. The pressure filled me with fear that my equipment wouldn't work, so I faked like I had to pee, and ran for the bathroom to get ready. When I got back, Neil was moving in, so I threw him out, got on top of her, and let instinct take over.

The next day we did it again. Then Neil and I returned the following week and sort of separately wound up with her. There was a pregnancy scare, and Neil and I spent hours on the phone trying to figure out what to do; which was good practice for him because a year later, when he was fourteen, another girl (who was thirteen) had his baby. I resolved never to have sex again. Never, ever, ever. And when, at last, the Debbie ordeal passed, I cried tears of relief - then I was off and running.

I fell hard for the next girl I was with, but when Mom intentionally walked in on us while we were naked, I lost her. It was probably good riddance, though, because she got me beat up by the football team.

My mother hired on as a stewardess for a tiny airline when I was fourteen. I was by myself a lot, and the nights alone were frightening. I started seeking out girls with impunity, and my unlimited freedom, combined with the heavy religious repression in that part of the country, made this search a fruitful one.

Nothing made me as happy as being with girls; and I felt like I was good for them too. My time with Mom had taught me that women were angels and men were beasts, and knowing this, and being sensitive to it, made me feel different from other guys. It gave me confidence too. I was totally comfortable approaching the fairer sex, and if they were going to save me the trouble, so much the better. I loved girls, all of them, and the more I could get to sign off on me, the less I needed my mother.

I am, however, sure that I was being reckless, especially toward the end of my time in Oklahoma; but I operated this way until Amarillo proved me wrong.

***

When I ran into April at Bourbon Street, she really was a virgin. I never would have believed this from a dancer, but she wasn't dancing. She was keeping time (basically, checking girls in and out of work, and tracking shift fees).

She had answered an ad in the paper while studying accounting at the U of A, and Joe Mack offered her the same job at our club when she transferred back.

We began dating almost immediately after reconnecting, and when the issue of her virginity came up, I thought at the very least I had some experience to offer, and not just in a general way. I'd been down this road with Andie, and it was one of the coolest moments of my life. I felt like I had respect for the situation too, because there were a couple of times when, in the heat of battle, a willing someone had told me that they hadn't gone all the way yet, and I'd turned back. The only problem was, I really didn't trust myself with nice girls anymore - for a multitude of excellent reasons - and April was one of the nicest people I had ever met.

ァ

THE WAR

My life has become a superhero's dichotomy, or perhaps a super villain's. By day, I am a mild mannered college student dating a virgin I met in high school; but at night, while the good people of the city sleep, I become The Great Libido, Guardian of the Dancing Whores.

No one has ever loved being surrounded by naked women more than me, but I also realize that people like April don't come along very often. And they are usually smart enough to spot a combustible situation when they see one. She has already talked about quitting - that is, her quitting, not mine - though she clearly wants us both to go. And, of course, we should. But part of me really wants to stay. Yeah, yeah - the dick part, right? Yes, certainly the dick part, but also the part that loves songs and books and movies about heartbreakingly fucked up situations. If that stuff interests you, then working here is like simultaneously watching and starring in a super-duper salacious movie. It's thrilling, and arousing, and for someone like me, it engages all of the senses.

There is something else too, though. Something I would never in a million years tell anyone for fear of being laughed at. It might sound ridiculous – it does sound ridiculous - but I really think I can help. Seriously. Like maybe there's someone in this room that I could save; someone I could search out the good in, and fix. Someone who would then be extremely grateful to me, and never, ever leave. I never realized how much I love the bird with the broken wing. Not the big fat, wallflower bird – I'm not Mother Theresa - but, you know, the exotic bird with lots of colors that maybe talks a little, and loves to fuck. Okay, my metaphor is crumbling, but I believe in this idea completely, and it makes me feel powerful, and almost good for being here. Kind of like a missionary or something.

Then I look at April, who needs no saving, and could probably rescue me from my delusions of grandeur if only I could inch a little closer to the light, and I wonder what in the hell is wrong with me. I truly wish I knew. I do know, however, that something has to give, because there is no room in anyone's life for both of these things.

I have reviewed the pros and cons, thoroughly.

April is incredibly cute and very smart, and I like myself when I'm with her. We smile a lot, and go to the movies, and talk about reading, and even hang out with her mom. She will make a superb mother some day, I'm sure of it, and I think she sees potential in me. Potential which, I fear, is not there; or, more precisely, potential that is shrinking under a long, black cloud of my own making. I wish sometimes that she would just go away so I wouldn't have to think about this stuff. It was so much easier being an outcast, at least I could deal with my feelings in private. I am a walking disappointment, and I want to warn her in the worst way. To just shake her and scream, "Are you fucking blind! Can you not see the horns sticking out of my head!" And when we talk about her impending first sexual experience, and my role in it, I cringe, and I want to say, "Look, I'm flattered, but don't you ever ask yourself why I've fucked so many girls? And what on earth makes you think I've come to a titty bar to stop screwing around?" In these moments, her belief in me, or willingness to offer a clean slate, is enraging. I feel like I'm boxing with a toddler, or bringing a bazooka to a pillow fight. How can she look at me and see Danny from "Grease," when I'm obviously fat, stinking Ron Jeremy inside. I just don't get it.

But then I try to remember that I am young enough, at least theoretically, to change. And if you took away the steroids, my life while the sun is up seems remarkably close to wholesome. I eat right, I don't drink anymore, I get plenty of robust exercise, and I love my baby sister. I am, in these hours, proof of God's amazing capacity to extend second chances; because after all of the drunkenness, and lust, and cruelty, and destruction, and theft, and violence, and vandalism, and disobedience, and truancy, and wanton disturbing of the peace, I may be just a few Dianabol away from being an All-American boy.

Now if I could just walk away from the nighttime, where the music is loud, the emotions are extreme, and the dirtiness I feel is trumped by the girls who come on like a ton of bricks, then maybe everything would be fine. I want to do the right thing, I really do, but the devil on my shoulder thinks that I could almost have my pick of girls in here. And maybe not almost. For instance, a dancer named Sindy was watching me the other day. I smiled at her, and about fifteen minutes later, her girlfriend came up and said, "You know, she really wants to get fucked by you." I said something like, "Oh…," and then she hung around as if we were going to set up a lunch date or something. It's always like that. This one wants a ride home, and that one wants to tell you about a gangbang she had, the other one thinks you're cute, and the one with the bleach blonde hair grins and takes her bottoms down in front of you just to fluster. Would any of these people be good for me? Of course not. Most of them are cheating on the boyfriends they already have; but once in a while someone will seem sincere, if there is such a thing as sincerity in a den of iniquity.

I want April, and I want to want her even more than I do. It's just hard to hear that tiny whisper over the guttural roar of lust I expose myself to night after night. And now there is Ttina, who may have the most bewitching ass I have ever seen; and sweet mother of Zeus does she know how to shake it. She is eighteen, but she has this tall boyfriend who drops her off, and he looks to be about thirty. Fuck, why does she smile at me? She never smiles at anyone. And why does it seem like *Simply Irresistible* is playing every time she gets on the stage by the door? Thank God I have a few days off, because I feel like I'm at a crossroads, and I really need to think this through.

8

EMILY

When I want to remember that the world doesn't suck, and that there may still be unconditional good inside of me, I spend a day with Emily. She's three now, so I can take her to the movies and she will usually sit through it if I buy her some popcorn and a Coke. We have to watch a kids' show, but that's a small price to pay for some truly excellent company.

We almost didn't get in today, though, because I lied at the box office and said that Emily was two; and as they handed me the free little kid's ticket, she shouted, "No Craigy, I'm three!" I turned red, and the ticket lady laughed, and now we're watching the latest Disney movie involving a wild animal kept as a pet. This one's about a cheetah and a cheerful English family living in Africa, but these things always play out the same way. The cute, playful critter is fun to have around until it becomes an adolescent, then it gets ornery, and bad guys appear looking

119

to exploit or kill it. The kids try to save the cheetah, and the parents realize it must be returned to the wild. Then, in the end, the teary eyed family chases their creature friend toward the wilderness, and force a smile as they watch it run free, usually with another of its kind.

I must confess that after an hour and a half of this, my mind is wandering. I'm going to see April tonight, and I think we're supposed to do the nasty. This is making me terribly nervous, but I don't know why. I've been having sex for years, and never had a major problem (at least not in the execution of the act). It's just so much pressure. What if it sucks? What if I suck? Then she'll hate intercourse for the rest of her life and it'll be all my fault. Or maybe I'll get her pregnant and wreck things for her that way. Or maybe it will be great, who knows.

This movie definitely blows, though. It's the last reel of this nonsense, and the music is blaring so you'll know to be sad with the kids as they cry and throw rocks at the stupid cheetah. And now the slightest change in the score to signal a new emotion that the actors and script aren't capable of conveying; it's still sadness, but more of a happy sad, because a lady cheetah has just appeared in the distance. The cheetah looks back one last time. Is that a smile, or just a nod to say, "Don't worry, human children, I understand that you only want the best for me, and I will never forget you." Then, as the cheetah sprints majestically across the savanna toward its future mate, a complete switch from musical pathos to exuberant exultation of the glory of life, and its ever-changing bullshit.

Oh, come on. Have the producers of this dreck no shame! Uch, what hacks.

I'm ready to leave in a fit of cynical disgust when Emily turns to me with tears in her eyes. She's been sitting on my lap for most of the movie, and I guess I've forgotten to check in with her.

"Why does the cheetah have to go, Craigy?," she says, and my heart melts. Damn, I was totally wrong about this movie. It is awesome, and I am jerk for feeling like a genius just because I've seen a few of these things. "It's okay, Petunia," I tell her, and give her a big hug. She needs answers now, and she looks into my eyes like I really, no kidding around, know exactly why the world works the way it does. Of course I do not, but grown people have an enormous responsibility in moments like these. So I sweep the cynicism from my face, and explain that when cheetahs grow up they want to be around other cheetahs, and that he will be happy now, and have his own baby cheetahs some day.

That's good enough for Emily; and though she is still a little tearful when we leave, our day together has been an enormous blessing, like it almost always is.

I drop her off at Mom's, and she kisses me on the cheek and says I love you. There isn't another human being on the planet that I would buy this from, but I absolutely believe her. And finally, I have a little peace of mind too, because even though I can't draw a clear line from this moment to tonight with April, it makes me feel like maybe, just maybe, everything will be okay after all.

9

THE VOYAGE

Vaseline melts condoms on contact. I had no idea because I almost never use them. I was just trying to make the whole thing a little easier. Which obviously means that it wasn't okay. I sucked, worse than I have ever sucked in my entire life. I feel so bad for her, but there was just nothing there, chemistry-wise. It was sort of like taking someone sailing who has never sailed before. You're out in the middle of nowhere, everything is going along fine, and then the wind just disappears. The boat works fine. It totally floats, and it is absolutely a perfectly handsome and seaworthy craft; but nature just isn't providing that spark you need to drift away and really get into the sailing. And now you are stuck, miles from shore, and your guest is looking at you like, "You know what you're doing, don't you?"

"Of course, of course," you smile, as you whip out an oar and start paddling. The sun beats down, and your every move is being studied, so you resort to nautical jargon in an attempt to reassure. "Starboard, port, crow's nest..." you ramble, but she just keeps on staring, with big curious eyes, wondering what in the hell you are up to, until, eventually, a gentle breeze returns, and somehow you get the ship into harbor.

Back on dry land, at last, you exchange pleasantries, share a clumsy hug, and after a long, awkward moment, she leaves, wondering why anyone would ever want to mess around with a boat.

***

I sent flowers the next day, hoping to assuage the profound disappointment that I was sure she must have been feeling; and to my complete surprise she said she wanted to do it again. So we did it again, a few more times, but I always felt like Dr. Mengele performing a procedure on an overly trusting naked person. She seemed happy, though, and her mother seemed happy, and my mother seemed happy, and everyone knew about the sailing. There was something in the air too; maybe not marriage, but an outsized and premature feeling of great goodwill. Then April quit the club, and I felt like she was taking me sailing. I didn't have another job to jump into, and I was also up to my eyeballs in temptation, so resigning my post at the naked lady emporium became one of those things that you are definitely meaning to do, but never get around to. And every night there was Ttina, with her superfluous T and two French last names, always smiling, and making me look like a rock star to the other guys who worked the door. I liked her stage name too; Jolene, which I mistakenly thought was a nod to the Dolly Parton song where Dolly, in the first person, begs a much sexier woman not to take her man. I have always loved that tune. I just never thought I'd be living it.

I resisted. I tried to be fully present when I was with April, and I intended with all my might to quit that job. But then one night after work, I wound up at one of the other bouncer's houses. Ttina showed up with a couple of her girlfriends, and they took off their tops and went swimming in the g-strings they wore at the club. This time, however, there were no Band-aids or pantyhose; and the water washed away their make up, Aqua Net, and perfume. I couldn't believe how much better she looked without all of that crap, but it definitely wasn't leading me in the right direction. So I got up, walked inside, found an unplugged electric guitar and started playing. I thought maybe I could gather my thoughts the way I used to when I first got to Edmond; but piddling around with the three chords of "Simple Man" wasn't getting me anywhere. I decided to leave, or at least stand up and think about leaving; but when I turned around Ttina was there, watching me - only this time she wasn't smiling.

PART THREE

THE ROAD TO

CALIFORNIA

(With a Few More Hours in New Mexico)

1

THE ROLLER COASTER

I am standing in the shadow of a rickety, wooden roller coaster, looking out at the Pacific Ocean. The sun is shining, the sky is blue, and even the bums digging in the trash look beautiful. It is so gorgeous, in fact, that I almost can't believe we're really here. It's like a dream come true. And since we drove all night to get out of the shitass desert, I'm going to enjoy this warm ocean breeze even if it is a mirage.

Mission Beach is an entire country away from the Atlantic coast of Florida, and the story of my parents, but I feel them right beside me because we used to vacation here. About fifty yards down the strand is the apartment we rented when my mom and dad were still married, and also the sand where Mary and I played. For years I've dreamed about returning to California, but what am I doing here now, with Ttina? Well, at the moment, trying not to tell her what I'm thinking; which is, if the sky broke open, and God

Almighty were to hurl fireballs at this collapsing carnival ride, that would be about the perfect metaphor for our relationship. Although, adding a swarm of flying monkeys and a plague of locusts would probably make it even more perfect.

It is truly amazing how fast you can lose everything; then get a tiny bit back, and lose that; and then lose more and more, and so on, and so forth, until you wind up on the front end of about a decade's worth of burnt creditors and bad karma. And that's basically why we moved here last night, on a whim, and under cover of darkness, with a few hundred dollars that should have paid our rent, and an old Blazer stuffed with dirty clothes, an appallingly soiled futon, a weeks old Mr. Teenage Arizona trophy, and a credit rating that stinks worse than my gym bag. All of this, because we have run out of places in Phoenix to hide - from ourselves.

Nine months ago, I broke up with April in the parking lot of her mom's townhouse. It was a horrible thing, and I'm sure that when this storm passes I'll look back and feel even worse than I already do; but right now I need to find us a place to live before the sun goes down; which is the fourth time that I have been in this particular situation since Ttina and I began our star-crossed, jealousy-fueled, alcohol and steroid binging, dysfunctional love affair.

The ugly truth is, I am a sex junkie now, raving and unrepentant, and nearly alone in the world. Ttina is all that I have left. She is my best friend and drug of choice, and I probably love her more than ever.

***

It seems like a lifetime ago that I was riding off to the strip club in Dad's car, high on his drugs and flush with his funds, but it has only been three years. The time in between has been like reading "The Grapes of Wrath," then all of the sudden realizing that you have become Tom Joad, limping your loved ones down the highway in a broken down jalopy at the blazing peak of the Dustbowl. And that is too grandiose, because it's really more like I am Oliver Hardy and my dick is Stan Laurel. Or maybe my brain is Moe, and my heart and penis are Larry and Curly. I don't know; I just love to fuck my girlfriend, and I've sort of dedicated my life to it.

Within a month of walking into Ttina's apartment for the first time, everything had changed. First, Mom threw me out of her house for leaving my virginal girlfriend for a lusty striptease artist. It was not a proud day, but I just drove down the street and moved in with Ttina. Then Bourbon Street fired me for openly dating a dancer. Again, fine, because I couldn't stand to watch her strip anymore. But soon college was gone too because I couldn't focus on my studies knowing that she was getting naked in a roomful of strange guys. I still had the gym, though, and I was working at that harder than ever, but at night I'd sit in her empty apartment and stare at the walls. I'd try to read, but I couldn't. There was no television to watch, so I'd go out for a long walk and be back in ten minutes. Sometimes my friends and I would hang, but since I wasn't drinking anymore this would only last a short while. Then I'd be back in her living room, pacing or doing push-ups in front of a wall sized mirror until two in the morning, when Ttina would return with her bag of costumes, a couple sacks of junk food, and a tackle box crammed with make-up and money - which roughly equaled my paycheck for an entire week of bouncing. We'd eat, screw, and then sit around giggling like little kids at a slumber party - minus the parents, plus hours upon hours of intercourse.

I felt I'd found a kindred spirit with a similar, but harder, story to tell. And it was good to feel such a blazing attraction for someone I didn't have to explain myself to. This was truly the era of happiness, the salad days, the good times, the two and a half weeks of quasi-innocence before she got comfortable enough to drink around me. Then a whole new person emerged – Ttipsy Ttina.

The first time I met Ttipsy Ttina, she was topless and twirling her hair in the crotch of a car salesman. The DJ was blasting that excruciatingly awful Poison song which goes, "I want action tonight, satisfaction all night," and it was slowly dawning on me that watching the girl I love get naked in public was never going to work, when Ttanya, Ttina's best friend since girlhood, approached. She said they were leaving early and wanted to borrow my car until I got off. This sounded more like a warning than a request, and I was going to refuse anyway because I knew they'd been sneaking drinks in the dressing room; but when Ttina walked up to me in street clothes, I relented. I just couldn't watch her take her top off again – or rather, I could not bear to watch other guys watch her take her top off again.

I handed Ttina the keys, and as I did, Ttanya looked at me like I was the dumbest nut she had ever met. Ttina kissed me on the way out the door, and for an instant I felt like things might be okay. Then, less than a minute after they left, the car salesman followed them out.

Denial and I were becoming fast friends. I wasn't asking questions I should have asked, and I was ignoring things no sane person would have ignored. Something like, "God will provide," or, "Man, if she wrecks my car maybe she will love me even more," was going through my head. And I kept that record going full blast until closing time, when Ttina returned, missing the parking lot entrance with an entire half of my car, bouncing over the curb, then a cement barrier, and skidding to a stop at a slant about twenty yards beyond me.

A quick glance at my fellow bouncers told me my rock star days were officially done. In their eyes, I had become a different musician altogether – the whorehouse piano player, in love with the busiest girl in the joint.

But really, I was just me, dragging an S.E. Hinton ideal of love into a Traci Lords reality. And Ttina was just Ttina, a damaged girl who had been on her own since she was fifteen, staggering toward me, clearly hammered, and obviously intending to fake like I had done something wrong in the hopes that I would end up apologizing. This was an old game of my mother's, so I just shook my head and took the keys. I wanted also to express my profound disappointment and anger, but Ttanya was there, giving me the "I told you so," grin, and waiting to see what would happen next.

Of course Ttanya was well aware of what would happen next. She had been living with Ttina since they were freshman, when they both dropped out of high school and started dancing at a club in Albuquerque. She knew her well, and had watched more than a few of these relationships develop – and had even participated in a few.

Ttanya had my number from day one, but I had hers too. She was obviously in love with Ttina, and forever waiting out guys to get her back. There is a horrible Def Leppard song which starts out, "When you make love, do you look in the mirror? Who do you think of, does he look like me?" And when Ttanya told Ttina that this song reminded her of her, I had final confirmation on the issue. But it was crystal clear already, and I had no intention of giving up. I had already bet the farm on this relationship, and failure was not an option. To the contrary; I felt dared, and I wanted to scream, "You may think you know a thing or two about a thing or two, lady, but I happen to have the power of love on my side, and you just watch my magic work!" This would have sounded ridiculous in the middle of the slurring tirade of fraudulent, ass covering, recriminations Ttina was aiming in my direction, so instead, I threw a mighty glare at Ttanya filled with every bit of this meaning and more.

She responded with a smile that said, "Oh, I wouldn't miss your magic show for the world." Then she winked, and walked inside to borrow a joint and take a piss.

2

HOME, SWEET HOME

In Phoenix, the standard young stripper's home is a
"luxury" apartment designed to resemble a French cottage
inside of a sprawling Spanish mansion. It is a one or two
bedroom with vaulted ceilings, new appliances, brassy fans,
maybe a useless fireplace, and bathrooms with "lavish
appointments." Her neighbors are restaurant managers,
workaday realtors, divorced people taking a step down,
corporate strivers on their way up, and the occasional
bachelor auto mechanic with panache. She will, however,
rarely run into these people because they move around in a
different half of the day.

In the early afternoon, while she sleeps, you can walk
out on the patio and look down at the pool. If it's summer,
the deck will be clean and the water blue and empty. It is
usually too hot to sit outside in the daytime, so people
avoid the swimming area until night. Then, depending on
the hour and the day of the week, there may be a tired dad

watching his kids splash around, or an El Lame-o party in the clubhouse. And when the bar crowd rolls in, you might even catch someone having sex in the hot tub. But in the hours between noon and three, you've got it all to yourself. Which makes this a good place to gather your thoughts; although fifteen minutes is about the limit because the patio, like everything else, is scorching hot while the sun is shining.

Back in her living room, you confront the lone piece of furniture – an entertainment center, rented to own. The interest rate on this wildly overpriced stack of particle board is hellacious, and it will never be owned. Nor will it ever house a television, or a stereo, or any other piece of entertaining electronica, because that stuff is expensive, and there is always something else to pay for.

In the corner is a cat box which hasn't been emptied in a week. A trail of litter leads into the kitchen, where the cat - almost always a kitten of less than six months - is nosing at old take-out containers in the sink.

The second bedroom is also empty, with a mirrored closet door that makes it seem even more so. Her girlfriends occasionally stay here when they are between places, or boyfriends, or just too drunk to leave. And when they do, they huddle on the floor under the blanket that covered your bed in the sixth grade.

The master suite is where she sleeps; on an old futon beside a pile of once or twice worn mall clothes, and last night's accumulation of currency – ones, fives, tens, and twenties, folded twice and stained with lipstick.

If you care for her, looking at those bills is tough, because, despite her protestations, they represent a major compromise of your intimate life.

You go round and round about this:

"It's just a job!"

"But you're naked!"

"I'm just topless."

"Just topless?"

"Yeah, what's the big deal?"

"It's a huge fucking deal. As a matter of fact, it is the entire deal between a man and a woman."

"My tits?"

"Well.. yes, nudity, intimacy, making someone else feel good in a way that only the two of you should share."

"It's just my fucking tits!"

"Well, Joe and the bouncers come in there when you are totally naked."

"And you know that because you're a bouncer and you've seen all the girls naked. So are you intimate with them now?"

There are quieter versions of the same maddening talk, and sometimes she tells you she hates it and wants to quit. And occasionally she does quit, until the money runs out, and then she goes back again. Or maybe she'll hire on part-time at the tanning salon or the flower shop. A couple days a week is a start, and a reason to feel like a change is being made. But soon the reality of seven dollars an hour before taxes sets in, and the motivation to wake up early is difficult to conjure when you made three hundred bucks the night before. From this perspective, regular jobs seem ridiculous. They pay next to nothing, and are much harder to get and hold. You are not the center of attention, and the attention you do get, even if it's polite and sincere, feels positively muted by comparison. Then you have to be on time, take orders, work a fixed schedule and long hours, and on and on.

The truth is, she can't quit. And when you're sitting here, next to this sleeping girl whom you already know too well, that's really hard to accept. You wonder why she parties so much. You wonder why you are not enough. You wonder why love is not enough. And maybe years later, you realize that people who trust love don't wind up working in strip clubs. There is a common thread. A tragic past. It kills you to know her story, and those details tear at you worse than your own bad memories. And all of this anguish really only enables you to feel sad, or powerless, or angry, or frustrated, because in the end you can't change anyone who isn't ready to change – especially yourself.

3

PRELUDE TO OLYMPUS

Thank God for bodybuilding. It keeps me sane and gives me a sense of direction. Here lately, it also keeps me employed. People think it's ridiculous, and they are, for the most part, correct. There is rampant egotism in the gyms, and full tilt male vanity; and I am not immune. I shave my legs and chest, and have spent more time in tanning beds than I care to admit. Then there are the steroids, which shrink your nuts while you are on them, but actually make your dick a little bigger over the same period of time. Everything goes back to normal when you jump off, though, provided that you do jump off at regular intervals. You probably shouldn't drink or take stimulants while you're on them either, though plenty of people do.

With regard to the primary effects and side effects; you get bigger and stronger in a hurry, and the testosterone makes you horny as a jackrabbit. All good stuff; however, you will probably grow hair where you don't want it, and lose hair where you do. There will also be acne, and a very good chance that you will lose your temper and find it hard to get back. So is it worth it? For me, yeah. Chicks dig big guys, and people get out of your way. I also like how I look, and I enjoy the competition and camaraderie. I'm proud of my accomplishments; and make no mistake, competing in bodybuilding shows is an accomplishment. If you're doing it right, you'll spend three or four hours a day in the gym, minimum, and obsess over your diet like an anorexic debutante.

I've put on about eighty pounds since I started five years ago, and I feel in a lot of ways like a different person. And man, did I want to be a different person.

It all started with Jenny, back in Edmond. When we were freshmen she was boning this inbred piece of shit on the football team; which ordinarily wouldn't have been a problem, but she was still my girlfriend. I probably saw the writing on the wall on this one. Mom had accidentally/on-purpose walked in on us while we were upstairs, naked in my bed. Maybe I was getting too comfortable having the house to myself, but the door was closed, and Mom definitely has some weird boundary issues. Anyway, she ordered Jenny and me into the car and drove her straight home (easily the longest ride of my life).

From that point on, my days with Jenny were numbered, but an official heads-up would have been nice. Instead, I got the news from Clenis (a combination of Claude and penis that Leigh and I concocted as my defense mechanism) when he stomped my ass at a Mid-High game. Mom was out of town, so I ran home, hid in my room, turned off the lights, and screamed along with the stereo.

They say that the road ain't no place to start a family. Right down the line it's been you and me. And lovin' a music man ain't always what it's supposed to be...

Oh Journey, why don't you write songs for fourteen year-old boys who get beat up at football games?

Such is life, I guess.

When I was done screaming, I realized that I had to reinvent myself. Every time I saw Claude he started something, and before long his asshole friends began doing the same. And Jenny, who was one hundred times the cunning, adolescent Joan Collins I took her for, would just smile and smack her gum in her braces as she walked by with her hand on the Skoal can in his back pocket.

To be fair, though, it wasn't just Jenny. The Ray thing was getting worse, being skinny always sucked, and I was really uncomfortable with getting my ass kicked all the time.

I made a deal with Mom on my fifteenth birthday. "Let me stay home today and I will go to the gym with Ray." It was a grim negotiation carried out in their room while they were in bed together. The sight of them made me want to barf, but desperate times call for desperate measures, so I forced a smile and lobbied hard until I got what I needed.

On the way over, I picked Ray's brain; an operation which ordinarily bore precious little fruit, but the gym was a passion of his, and he seemed to know what he was talking about, so I decided to swallow my pride and take a little direction. I did not want to look like him, though. He was wearing a tank top – as usual - and his flabby barrel chest held little aspirational appeal. Still, he was big, and there was no doubt that he, like almost everyone else in town, could kick my ass. As a matter of fact, he, like nearly everyone else in town, had kicked my ass.

4

THE SUMMER OF GAINS & LOSSES

At the International Fitness Center, the French lady behind the counter (the only evidence of anything international) asks, "Will you be working out with your brother today?" My mom teaches aerobics here, and this lady knows that Ray is not my brother, but I nod in the affirmative anyway.

Edmond is Baptist country, so shorts are not allowed on the workout floor. And since shorts are what I am wearing, I fear my self-improvement mission may be over before it begins. Happily, though, there is nothing to worry about. A loaner pair of baggy sweats is pushed across the counter, and with that, and a wave of the French lady's hand, we are in.

"The Floor" is a two story, carpeted warehouse packed with exercise apparatus. A suspended jogging track hangs overhead, and there is the damp smell of mildew, sweat, and chlorine. It is dark, and because there is no music, the clang of machines and a circuit training tape predominate.

The recording encourages; "Ready begin... Thirty more seconds... Almost there... Stop and check your pulse."

At capacity, this place may hold three hundred people, but this morning there are just a few grimacing housewives, some kids from the college, and plodding truck driver with a big gut, mangy whiskers, and pasty skin. Ray wants to get right to it, but I'm still taking in the fluorescent lights, fake palm trees, and thatched hut full of tanning beds, when a uniformed trainer approaches. I know him. His name is Cory, and he is the adult son of the married manager my mom used to bone. He offers to show me around, and while we are in the snack bar, which proudly serves Levi Garrett chewing tobacco, protein shakes, and cheeseburgers, he asks me if his dad has been sneaking over to our house at night. I look through the glass wall to the pool area and decide to tell him the truth. Cory is a decent guy, and I'd want a straight answer if I was him. He is not surprised by my response, and I sense that we have both lived with our share of parental infidelity.

We chat a little more as we walk upstairs through the locker rooms, and into a mirrored area where you can analyze your body from every conceivable angle. However, the angle I am used to is painful enough, so I decide to avoid this room for the time being.

Cory sizes me up and finds much room for improvement. I am 6'0, 135 lbs with a dismal fourteen percent body fat. I wonder if I am a skinny fat guy or a fat skinny guy, and also whether the bargain I struck to skip school was worth it. This is humiliating, and I'd much rather be sleeping in Spanish class; but the current version of me is unacceptable and I seriously need to fix what needs fixing.

It is May and school lets out in three weeks. My pledge is a new life by September, which means no more guitar, no more friends, no more movies and concerts, and no more girls until I am who I want to be. I stay home all summer and gorge myself. Lunch becomes a death march to the brink of vomiting - four or five hamburgers washed down with a blender-sized milkshake. Breakfast and dinner are similar ordeals. Severe limitations in my knowledge of bodybuilding nutrition are compensated for by six mile round trip walks to the gym, often twice a day.

In a single week, I read every muscle building text at the Central State Library. There are two: the Nautilus Bodybuilding Book and a companion volume to the documentary "Pumping Iron." Here I encounter my new hero, though I have already met him in the movies. His name is Arnold, and he is a man without limits.

I love Arnold's movies, but only because they feature images of Arnold; and I am intoxicated and inspired by his story. Surely if he can go from obscure Austrian immigrant to undefeatable bodybuilding champion, real-estate mogul, movie star, and Kennedy husband in just fifteen years, I can use his methods to protect myself from Ray and a bunch of teenage football rednecks. Of course, this is bad news for Keith Richards, Eddie Van Halen, and John Lennon, whom I will always love; but a bunch of skinny rock stars can't help me with my current problems, and the Austrian Oak would snap them like twigs. So, after a period of intense soul searching on this matter, I send all of my once and future music heroes to the back of the Schwarzenegger

Super Rocket of Boundless Possibility, and strap myself in for take-off.

Arnold teaches me to have goals, and to visualize the man I want to be as I am lifting weights. I obey, and in these visions I see myself as an invincible mountain of muscles whom no man dares cross, and no woman dares leave. I am a holy warrior marching to the top of Mount Olympus, where I will install a more benevolent order, and enforce it with a zealot's vengeance. Arnold is already up there, urging me on to that better place. "More weight!" he commands, "More reps! You will only succeed only when you want it worse than anyone. Vil you vant it - vil you!"

"Yes, Arnold," I scream between my ears, as I push the cold metal bar off my chest. "I vil, I vil, I vil!"

***

It is late June, the end of my first month of solitude and transformation. No one is calling me, and I am calling no one, but my goal is always foremost in my mind. I am tough, I can handle this. I'm already up to 150 lbs. Mom and Ray are still nuts, but being stuck under the same roof with these people doesn't mean I have to live with them. There is a television in my room, so I can sit in here and watch the Olympics. And since Mary has moved back to Florida, they will have the whole rest of the house in which to maul each other.

Now Ray is knocking at my door. He wants the TV I'm watching. He and Mom are going to bed.

"You can go into the living room and watch now," he says.

"But I don't want to," say I.

"I'm taking it."

"No you're not."

He walks over and unplugs the television, and I, holding a miniature guitar, stand up and tell him to go away. He pushes me. As I fall backwards onto the bed, the mini-guitar swings up and catches him in the nuts. He goes berserk, doubles up his fist and cracks me in the face three or four times. He pins my arms with his legs and screams in my face. I yell for Mom. She is standing in the hallway, but she does nothing.

"He hit me in the sack!" yells Ray.

"Mom, help!" I plead.

"Well, you probably deserve it." She says.

I get loose and run upstairs to Mary's old room and call the police. Within minutes they are at the front door. Mom and Ray walk outside with them, but they never ask to see me. I'm not sure why. In Oklahoma we do not spare the rod for risk of spoiling the child. Perhaps that is why. I also have a growing record of misdemeanor offenses ranging from public drunkenness to petty theft to auto burglary and curfew violations. Mom digs into her bag of tricks to get rid of the cops. I get the dirtiest of looks from her and Ray. Then the television disappears.

The next day Mom is on the phone spinning a version of the story with me as the instigator. Within a week there is a letter from Dad telling Ray that he knows that I am hard to deal with and that he should feel free to use whatever measures he deems necessary to discipline me.

***

Onward to July. I am up to 160 lbs, and Grandma is dying. She has cancer. It went away for a while, and we thought she was cured. Then it came back.

As the barbells and milkshakes make me bigger, extreme doses of chemotherapy and disease waste her away. Grandpa and Tommy are in shock. They walk around in a daze. Everyone does. It has never been clearer that she is the sun that our family revolves around. When she is gone there will be no compassionate center keeping everyone in touch with everyone else. There will be no place that everyone calls home. There will be nowhere that everyone is on their best behavior. Oklahoma itself will lose its luster. Grandpa will have no Grandma, and Tommy will have no mom.

Watching her go is horrible. She lies on the couch where I threw up a year ago after an eighth grade bender. She can't run around anymore. She can't cook for us. She can't love us. She is too stoned, and weak, and sick. Her hair comes out in clumps. She keeps a brave face when she is aware, but there are lapses when she cries. She is in and out of the hospital. We keep moving and hoping and denying until it is obvious. Then she is back in the hospital for the final time. She is fifty-nine. Mom and I are in her room. Diane is down from Pennsylvania, and Cheryl is here from Paul's Valley. For a little while Grandma is fine, then she is confused. She is pulling out her hair and crying. It is frightening. Mom and Diane look at me. They are scared. I am terrified. They order me to leave. I don't know what to do. It is only fifteen feet or so to the door, but it feels like miles.

"I love you, Grandma."

"I love you too," she says. Then the door closes. It feels like everyone is staring, but no one is around. I walk into the stairwell, climb to the top and fall apart.

I am immediately sent to Dad's for a "vacation."

It is the middle of the afternoon, two days after my arrival, and Dad has been totally cool. We've eaten out every meal and gone to the movies. But now we are alone in the hallway and he has a strange look on his face. "Your grandmother passed away." He hugs me.

"Do you want to go back?"

"Yes."

"Okay."

I am on a plane the next morning. I arrive in the middle of the afternoon. In the short time that I've been away, my cat, Jaws, has been killed by a car. Poor Jaws. Ordinarily this would be devastating, but Jaws has been trumped. We go straight to Tommy's house. You can feel that Grandma is gone. There are a few sad faces, but no Tommy. I walk upstairs to his room. He is on the bed under the window, lying on his stomach. He looks like he's been kicked by an elephant. He says nothing. I lay down beside him.

***

In August, we bury Grandma. Grandpa is losing his grounding. Tommy is changing. Mom is sad. Ray is moving. In a week, I will be a sophomore in high school, and I weigh 170 pounds.

5

PLAYING HOUSE

I am fucking Ttina on the couch at Ttanya's apartment. My rival has retired to her chamber, but her door is open just a crack and I can feel her watching. A threesome is not out of the question – as a matter of fact, it is on the menu – but I've heard stories of the aftermath of their adventures in this arena, and I'd like to avoid my version of Ttina smashing up a trophy case or having an hours long hysterical crying fit. No, I'll keep playing this the way I've been playing it because I want to keep her, and help her if I can; and besides, I am winning – though I'm not entirely sure what this victory is buying me.

It has been a couple of months now, and I think sometimes our love is generating positive results. She quit dancing. Okay, she got fired for getting drunk at the club, but that scene is out of our lives now, and that can only be a good thing – right? She's looking for a real job too, and I just started at Max's 919. My first night was a Red Hot

Chili Peppers' show, and I consider that a good omen. However, there are some not so good omens too.

We are, essentially, homeless. A friend of mine loaned us her spare room, but we aren't paying rent, and Ttina's idle hands have not helped the situation any. Max's should give us a boost, but Ttina's retirement left a big hole in our finances, and I'm not sure how we're going to fill it. Nothing to worry about, though, because love conquers all. I still believe that, even if her drinking is a bit of a challenge. Okay, maybe more than a bit.

She comes to Max's to dance while I am working. Almost always she'll run to the top of the stairs and tell me that some guy is messing with her. I inevitably zip down and bark at someone, who generally seems baffled by my accusations. I need this job, so I've been sending my colleagues to handle these episodes lately.

But this is really just the pre-story, story. The one you tell a stranger to test the waters, before diving into the, "This guy might be insane," stuff. And here is the rationalizing bit: I am right on course for the Mr. Teenage Arizona contest. I'm focused, I've paid careful attention to my training, posing, diet, and tanning (all free because the gym is sponsoring me), and I think there's a good chance that I can win.

Great, so what's the problem?

Well, I guess the general tone of the thing.

The tone?

Um, Ttina won't leave me. We drove to Albuquerque a few weeks ago and I met her mother, grandmother, and little sister. And she didn't drink the whole time.

Great.

Yeah, and she didn't wear any make-up on that trip, either. We had some really good talks.

Sounds like things are headed in the right direction.

Yeah, she gave me a blowjob in the car the other night.

Okay...

I was driving, and there were two girls and a guy from work in the backseat.

Oh...

It was cool, though. It's just that the cops come over sometimes.

Really?

Yeah, when she gets drunk, she yells and throws punches.

That sounds...

Bad, I know. And a few times she has run out the door, screaming, and disappeared into the night. Once totally naked; though she was giggling hysterically then.

Oh...

But I don't chase her anymore. She comes back faster that way.

Whoa, look at the time!

It's simple psychology, really. Though I probably shouldn't loan her my car anymore. I had to work late a couple nights ago, and she didn't pick me up. It was 3:30 in the morning. I'd waved off all my friends, and eventually I just started walking. About a mile down the road, I was hitchhiking when a man picked me up. He said he was out "looking for chicks," and I ignored him because I was tired and just wanted to get home; but when he asked if I wanted to "give 'er a pump," I had the sneaking suspicion that something was up - and it was.

He was masturbating, so I grabbed him by the neck and he slammed on the breaks. Then I jumped out and marched the remaining couple of miles to our apartment. Ttina got there about fifteen minutes later, and the cops arrived about a half hour after that.

Listen, I should probably get going.

Oh, no problem at all, but I don't want to give you the wrong idea. She's a really good person, and I'm going to get her into college as soon as I go back. And it's more than sex, I swear. She reads; mostly horror crap, but she does read. And... She stuck her tongue in my ass a few times, and I think she's going to let me do her in the butt. Hello... Hello...

6

KICKING ASS

Bouncing for a living is mostly a lot of standing around. People come to the door, and if they're of age and not sloppy drunk, you let them in. Inside, you keep an eye on these same people, and the vast majority never cause a problem. In the early-going you may find yourself overcompensating and being needlessly rude or confrontational, but gradually you learn a few tricks to help diffuse tense situations.

I like to look at my watch. If someone is angry and their field of vision is starting to close around you, sometimes you can open it back up by checking the time in a very deliberate way. This sends the subliminal message that there will be a moment beyond the current one where all parties concerned will likely be grateful that they opted not to involve themselves in a fistfight. I think it also reminds the other guy that you are a human being, just like them, and a pretty relaxed and unintimidated one (because you are checking your watch, and obviously have your mind on other things).

Most confrontations end here, with perhaps a little voice raising from the trouble-making soul as he (or she) walks away. If you are the voice-raiser, then the other bouncers are probably lining up behind you, which also helps to end an impasse before it escalates.

Alcohol is the wildcard, though. And as everyone knows, people do stupid shit when they are drunk. At Max's we had a full-blown melee where the entire ground floor filled with people throwing punches. Some of our guys wound up at the bottom of piles, and the violence continued, full bore, for about ten minutes until the entire Tempe Police Department showed up to shut the club down and cart people away.

At the strip club one night, a closing time confrontation between two patrons spilled over into the parking lot, and a man ran over another man with a big old Cadillac, then backed up and ran over him again. The cops used to sit across the street picking off drunk drivers, and they were on the scene in the blink of an eye. The Cadillac man was taken directly to jail, and his victim went to the hospital with severe leg injuries.

Drunk people do not like to be told what to do, and they are often fearless and irrational. This leads to fights between customers (one about every week or two, depending on where you're working), and causes you to have to physically throw people out (almost nightly). There is a trick for this too: You just square up with the offending party, pop them hard in the shoulder, continue their momentum by spinning the other shoulder in the direction of the first, then bear hug them from behind (with arms pinned to their sides), pick them up off the ground, and heave them out the door, giving yourself plenty of time to react if they regain their balance and decide to come back at you. (They almost never do.)

I've seen bouncers beat drunks up pretty severely. I've seen drunks throw sucker punches at bouncers – some of which connected. I've had a knife pulled on me, and been threatened more times, and in more ways, than I care to remember. But most of the time it adds up to nothing. The other guys have your back, and if you're alone, then, God willing, you have friendly regulars who will jump in on your behalf, if needed.

It is boring work, with brief and infrequent episodes of violence. And perhaps the worst thing that has ever happened to me, physically, was getting bitten on the finger. I was breaking up a fight between two guys and an off-duty bouncer in the parking lot, when one of them got my finger in his mouth and started biting. Out of instinct, I stuck two fingers on my other hand into his eye socket, all the way to the second knuckle - and he kept on biting! God knows where this would have led, and thankfully I didn't have to find out, because three men in street clothes emerged from out of nowhere, flashing badges. They called in a couple of squad cars, and I went to the hospital and had my finger scrubbed out and dressed.

Come to think of it, there are a surprising number of cops hanging around bars.

There really isn't much more to tell about the violent side of it. Sometimes you'll throw out a belligerent jerk, and a crowd of people will cheer for you. And sometimes you throw out a belligerent jerk, and he'll hang around outside causing trouble. I lost my temper with one such guy. (Thank you, steroids.) He smacked a dancer in the V.I.P. lounge, and I took it personally because she was a friend of mine. Anyway, over the course of the next hour, I blew my top and wound up spending the night in jail. Amazingly, he (a pilot in the Saudi Air Force) was one of my cellmates. I'd like to say that we became friends, but he was an even bigger dick as he sobered up - a real shitty human being.

Finally, my advice to any aspiring bouncer would be, try with all of your might to avoid getting in between couples when they are fighting – especially if they are drunk. Even if the man doubles up his fist and punches the woman, beware, because she will likely jump on your back and try to claw your eyes out as you are attempting to rescue her. You probably have to offer help in this situation, but it is a good idea to be very careful and ready for anything.

Oh, and finally, finally; if you are tempted to swipe cover charges or collect bribes for letting people in ahead of the line, or maybe just exchange preferential treatment for financial remuneration, I'd say go ahead and do it. Everyone does, and you will never make your bills on your hourly wage alone.

Or better yet, just find a regular job and involve yourself with regular people. In the long run (and the not so long run) you'll be happier and healthier.

ㄱ

BURNING DOWN THE HOUSE

Our bedroom is crowded with Tempe firemen and Ttina is lying on the mattress with a grotesquely dislocated arm. She is drunk and screaming and crying; and because dawn is breaking, several of our elderly, early-rising neighbors have come to the door to witness the commotion. I had no idea this tiny, furnished, one-bedroom apartment could fit so many people; but there are at least a dozen emergency workers and their gear in here. I count eight or nine fire guys, a few cops, and a couple of EMT's, all glancing from her to me, trying to figure out who is crazier.

This level of shame and embarrassment is brand new to me, and I'm surprised that it can happen without your head shrinking into your thorax and exploding in some kind of atomic mega-blush. The sensation is so intense that it probably deserves its own word, but that will have to wait, because the firemen and cops want to confer with me.

You never really get used to the look of pity and disgust that these protector types offer when they take you aside to explain what's going to happen next. I certainly don't like it, but I am grateful for it, because this means that they believe me, and I am off the hook. And why shouldn't they believe me? I've given them the truth. Nine months in, I can pretty much deliver the story before it even happens. It begins: "She came home drunk and..."

This time the "and" is a familiar tale - to a point. I loaned Ttina my car to go to her job – Why I keep doing this I really can't say - and she came home at four in the morning. She was supposed to pick me up from work a couple of hours earlier; but, well, you know. I was asleep on the couch when she walked in, and wasn't even going to bother with a fight. Instead, I just shook my head and told her I was done. Then she started swinging.

She connected a few times, then I jumped up, caught her fist in the air, and spun her arm behind her back like we do at the office. After that, I marched her into the bedroom, shut the door, and told her to sleep it off. For about thirty seconds everything was fine; then the door burst open, she flew out swinging, and roughly the same thing occurred again.

On the third go round, her shoulder popped out of the socket when I caught her fist. I guess it was the abrupt reversal of momentum that did it, but in the moment, I couldn't make any sense of what I was seeing. Her arm was just hanging there, at a completely unnatural angle, and it looked like her skeleton was broken. It was terrifying, and she was screaming bloody murder, so I called 911 and prayed for the best.

Under the circumstances, I guess the best has happened, because the police are basically saying, "The ambulance can take her to the hospital for X amount of dollars, or you can drive her yourself." Ttina and I have no money, and won't even be able to pay the doctor, so there is really no decision to be made; I'm driving.

Once our houseguests pack up and leave, I walk her ever so gently across the landing and down the stairs - with neighbors staring the whole way - to the parking lot, where my car is still warm, and parked at an angle.

This is a perfect morning for a drive. The sun is shining and there's not a cloud in the sky. And maybe if I'd had a little sleep and she didn't reek of booze, and perhaps if her skeleton fit together in the normal way and every bump in the road wasn't sending her into a fresh fit of agonized sobs, then this might be the beginning of a beautiful day. But instead, I'm beginning to doubt my power to rescue. More than that, really; I wonder if my whole premise was flawed. Like maybe I am the bad guy. It's certainly possible. A quick scan of my memory bank generates some disturbing possibilities; but to be honest, it's hard for me to pick it all apart because the picture is so distorted and the sound is warbling and shrill.

I remember my mom's story about my grandfather coming home drunk and throwing my grandmother down the stairs. She wound up in a full body cast, and his drinking didn't slow for decades. I see Ray and my dad seething and yelling and hitting, and I wonder if I have truly broken that chain. And then there is the familiarity of this episode. There were times toward the end in Oklahoma when Mom and I would argue, and she would flip completely out and come at me singing; literally, like the fat lady in an opera, except without words or melody - and loud, really loud. Her eyes would get crazy, and she'd be slapping at me, and I'd have to turn sideways as I restrained her for fear of getting kicked in the balls.

Is it possible that I've managed to dodge this stuff without dragging any of it into my own life? God I hope so, but the nurses in the x-ray room are looking at me like I'm Ike Turner. And when Ttina is locked in the imaging booth alone, and she starts screaming, "My baby, my baby! I want my baby!" (meaning me), I realize that I am crossing another new frontier of humiliation. These emergency room ladies have seen it all, and even they seem confounded by the Tennessee Williams play I've drug into their place of business on a Sunday morning.

***

When at last we are back in the car driving home, it is stone silent. Happily, the x-rays were negative and Ttina's arm is back in its socket; but I am confused. How long are you supposed to wait after a trip to the hospital to break up with your girlfriend? Now feels about right; but guilt and the four weeks I have until the Mr. Teenage Arizona contest will probably keep me in place for the time being. Good Lord, I hope I win. As a matter of fact, I doubt that anyone has ever needed a local teenage bodybuilding title more. I've just got to get something – anything – going so that I can rebuild. But like any other addict – and by now it's clear that I am a full-blown sex junkie with romantic delusions - my mind plays tricks on me. "Maybe if you get her pregnant," it whispers, "then you can save her and have a family too." I've caught my body playing along with this

159

one, and I can only thank God and steroids for dropping my sperm count to almost nothing. Then it pleads, "She's sorry. She didn't mean to." Or, "She's trying; she's really, really trying."

And she is trying. It's just that she keeps getting fired for being drunk on the job, or not waking up in the morning. She'll throw drinks at the boss, or tell some customer to fuck off, and always there's a story about a guy getting handsy or abusive. I'm not even surprised anymore when she comes home from the bar, or the tanning salon, or the beauty parlor, or wherever she's been employed for the previous couple of weeks – or days. The result is always the same. And now she's waitressing at a topless bar; or at least I thought she was.

We aren't even a full week out of the emergency room when a chance call to her new job informs me that Ttina the cocktail waitress is actually Ttina the topless dancer. She denies it, but I've obviously caught her red handed; and that pretty much tears it. I'm breaking up with her; and this time she is sober, so she gathers her stuff (a couple of trash bags full) and calls a friend for a ride. And that is the last time I see her until I'm standing on stage at the show and spot her in the crowd.

8

ESCAPE

I won – by a single point - and now I am Mr. Teenage of all of Arizona. It's a good feeling, and I want to follow it up with some more achieving, but the two weeks since the contest have been a little bumpy.

On the night of the show, Tommy and I drove to Max's. Ttina tracked us over there and made sure to catch me catching her dancing with some strange guy in a suit and ponytail. I was about to leave when the DJ stopped the music, turned up the house lights, and made the announcement that I had just brought home the plastic at the small time bodybuilding contest, of which no one was even aware. A couple of cocktail waitresses woo-hooed, and then you could have heard a pin drop. The next five seconds went by like the trials of Hercules, as I stood there, surrounded by strangers who didn't even know where to look, silently praying for the man to turn the music back on so that I could sneak out without any of my co-workers noticing.

After that, Tommy and I went to Denny's and gorged. Then I went home and passed out.

Two days later I was sleeping with Ttina again, and five days after that we were having an all night crank bender, and telling the guys from work that we were going to get married when the sun came up. Once again, I can only thank God that drugs eventually wear off, and in this case, not a minute too soon.

But here we are once more – Ttina and I – in the apartment where we broke up for good less than a month ago. There's four hundred dollars cash on the coffee table that ought to go to the rental office, but once we drop that money off we're stuck here for thirty more days – and we probably can't make it that long without some big project or disaster to hold us together. So, because there are no more plausible, "It'll all work out," stories left to tell each other, we have decided to pack up our shit and move to California.

It is midnight, and because our recent crank adventure showed us that sunlight leads to momentum loss and unwelcome clarity of thought, we've decided to leave immediately; and from this decision flows the added benefit of being able to load up and skip town without alerting the onsite office manager.

Three hours into our journey, I am giddy, and she is giddy, and when the sun comes up we pull off the road in the middle of nowhere to fuck, right out in the open.

We park in the sand, on a turnout in the desert, and I take off my shirt. She opens the passenger door, smiles, and hikes up her skirt. Then we give the lizards a show as traffic whips by just a hundred yards away. If anyone cared to look backwards, they could easily see us, but no one does; and when we are finished, I stand there sweating, chugging from a water jug, and feeling freer than I have ever felt in my life. She drops her skirt back down, throws her panties in the back, and joins me on the rock where I am standing. We laugh and stare at each other like Bonnie and Clyde. We are young and good-looking, and though we are putting on some serious miles, it truly seems at the moment like the laws of society do not apply to us. I mean, we are doing it! We are really blowing off the world and going to California, and it is one of the best feelings I have ever had.

A couple of hours later, we sweep down through El Cajon and into San Diego County. It's all laid out there before us, and every sign with the words "San Diego" or "California" sends shivers down my spine, and fills me with steroidal thoughts of manifest destiny. It's so green, and the air is so clear and humid; and when we pass the blue observation tower at Sea World and the billboards for the San Diego Zoo, I want to scream "Thank you, God!" at the top of my lungs.

We arrive at the ocean late in the morning and spend the next hour just looking at it. Then, because it is getting late and we have nowhere to live, we drive up and down the coast chasing "For Rent" signs, before landing in a ratty apartment building on the strand in Mission Beach. We have to clear out when the season starts, but a furnished one bedroom with a view of the ocean is a major conquest, and we decide to celebrate with Diet Cokes and fried food at a happy hour in the bay. It is a sublime moment - a real victory after a year of endless ordeals - and we are both almost too giddy to speak. And when she gives me the Bonnie Barrow grin again, we race back to our new home and dive headlong into round two.

9

MARK

When Ttina and I took off for California, I was secretly hoping that I could track down my cousin Mark, who owns a comedy club in Pacific Beach (and several others across the country). Our ends of the family aren't close, but he's been a hero of mine since I was a little boy, and saw him on the Merv Griffin and Dinah Shore shows. To be honest, he wasn't super funny, but watching a family member on television made me feel like I was related to Elvis.

So, in the warm glow of a show business Jones I was nursing even in elementary school, I wrote a fan letter, and Mark responded saying that if we ever made it to Los Angeles, he'd take me backstage at The Tonight Show. And while being nine years-old hindered my ability to put that trip together, my mom and I did get to spend an afternoon with Jonathan Winters around then because he and Mark's dad, a flashy Oklahoma oil man who lived in La Jolla, were drinking buddies.

Still, meeting up with Mark seemed like a long shot. He lived in San Diego, but he traveled a lot, and I hadn't even told anyone I was in town. Plus, he still seemed kind of unapproachable to me.

Our common grandmother had a room in her house in Oklahoma City that was covered in family photographs, and the one that jumped out as you walked in the door was a picture of Mark from his days as an All-American diver at Princeton. In the photo, he is climbing out of a pool, looking muscular, happy, and victorious; basically, all of the things that any little boy wants to be. I absolutely loved that picture, but as I got older, the rest of his story seemed even cooler.

He earned a PhD in Psychology, and almost immediately gave it up to work the door at The Comedy Store in Hollywood. There were rumors too, about his strange dietary and religious practices, and no one was really sure if he was gay or straight. He (like most of the men in our family) had alcohol issues in his past, and perhaps best of all, my parents thought he was crazy; apparently because he visited them once in Florida, showed up late, ate only bread, then vanished in the middle of the night without so much as a note saying "good-bye."

Unfortunately, aside from this encounter - which happened when I was very young - I had only ever had one brief, in-person interaction with him. It happened one day out of nowhere, when the family grapevine started buzzing with news that Mark had shown up at our Grandmother's house and would be there for a couple of hours. I got Tommy to drive me over as soon as I heard, but by the time we arrived, the place was already packed with relatives;

which meant getting to know him was out of the question. Still, I did manage to wrangle a few minutes of face time; and for the next hour or so I stood across the room staring at him, and wondering why he had given himself a buzz cut - and perhaps also if the happy look in his eye was really some kind of mania.

You just never knew with Mark; nobody did. And this fact was whirling around my head as I approached the Improv on the morning after Ttina and I arrived in San Diego. I was scared, and wondering if maybe Mark really was crazy; and even if he wasn't, I definitely did not want to be rejected by a familial hero. I had also never been so close to the inner sanctum of show business. I'd worked some rock concerts and wrestling matches in Oklahoma, and encountered the odd celebrity in the nightclubs, but this was California; striking distance from the big time, and home to all of the heavy-hitter Hollywood types.

I took a deep breath and knocked on the glass door by the patio bar. A tall guy with long hair answered and told me that Mark wasn't in. However, when I said who I was, he showed me where Mark lived, and I walked over.

Mark's place was a small, rented duplex on the street behind the club. He didn't believe in owning property, but he had so many broken down Studebakers that he had begun giving them away as prizes in his "Laff-Off" competitions (As a matter of fact, there was a sedan like Kermit drove in "The Muppet Movie" parked behind the club that day).

I had barely gotten to his gate, when Mark jumped out and shook my hand. I was startled, and the first thing that struck me was how small he was. All these years, he'd seemed so much larger than life, almost mythic. And now that I was seeing him in person, I was shocked to find that he was a good three inches shorter and maybe sixty pounds lighter than me. He wasn't tiny, really; just average, almost perfectly so.

Our first real talk went by in a flash – or at least the first act did. He remarked on how big I'd gotten, then asked if I wanted to walk with him to the post office. We did, and that night he took Ttina and me to our first show at The Improv.

Right away, I was hooked. Instead of a rowdy, leering crowd, most of the people here were on dates or with family members, and they were all laughing and having a good time. It was comfortable, and as the night wore on, the vibe reminded me of a clubhouse or a big den.

The room really didn't seem like a bar at all. The floor was flat, but the rest of the place looked more like a tiny black and white theater than a nightclub. I also loved how bright it was. The south wall was made of opaque glass brick, so even after the house lights went down, the hazy incandescence of neon signs and passing headlamps shown in. The effect was almost psychedelic; and when combined with the headshots of famous comedians on the other walls, it made me feel like I'd died and gone to the circus. And that was before the show even started.

We probably could have left after dinner and still counted the evening a huge success, because forty-eight hours earlier, Ttina and I were the deservedly disparaging talk of a shitty apartment complex in the suck ass desert. And now here we were, sitting at the raja's table, eating the first nutritionally sound hot meal we'd had in weeks, and receiving polite nods and small talk from the people who stopped to kiss Mark's ring. And when the headliner – a guy we recognized from the Letterman Show – came by to chat, we were beside ourselves with excitement. It was like a dream. We were just trying to run away from our problems, and somehow we'd fallen through the wardrobe into Narnia and hit it off with Aslan, the magical lion.

Mark's charm and generosity made me want to be just like him, and the proximity and apparent approval I was getting had me thinking that some of my wildest dreams might actually be achievable. I began, right then and there, to study his every move, making mental notes; and the first thing I was impressed with was his clear discomfort with the "boss man" attention he was getting. That attribute seemed like a keeper to me, though I wasn't sure why anyone would want to avoid having his ass kissed. He also didn't drop names, even when pressed; something else that I would totally have done had I been in his position. And when the emcee came on, and Mark angled himself away from the aisle so that people wouldn't bug him during the show, I did the same, even though there was absolutely no need for me to do so.

The performance started with a music cue, and a back of the house introduction, and the next ninety minutes were like a two hundred person magic carpet ride.

The rhythm of it all was fascinating. During the set-ups, the audience would float in anticipation of the punch lines, then laughter would explode like a bomb and swirl around the room in waves, as attention gradually refocused on the comic on stage. I'd seen this basic dynamic on television, but being part of the energy in the room was the difference between watching porno and having sex. Everyone was so involuntarily joyful, and until the checks dropped it seemed almost like time was standing still.

When it was over, I absolutely knew what I wanted to do with my life. Or rather, I knew that I'd never be happy sitting behind a desk, or selling something, or fixing things, or buying them for others. And I also knew that because Mark had done it, and we came from the same place and had the same grandparents, there was at least a fighting chance that I could too – if I could somehow find a way to pull my head out of my ass.

10

20

Yesterday was my twentieth birthday. I spent the morning at the gym, and in the afternoon, Ttina and I went down to the pier in Pacific Beach. We got a couple of corn dogs, and bought matching puka shell bracelets. It was one of those moments when God, or whatever, says, This is important, take a mental picture and save it. So I did; with her standing by the weathered wooden railing. The water was behind her, and the wind was blowing her hair just slightly. She was smiling and had the softness in her eyes that always makes me wonder how life might have been for her if she'd had normal, loving parents.

We sat there on a bench near the fishermen and she said she was thinking about dropping the extra T in her name. Then I told her I was thinking about going back to Arizona and enrolling in college. She didn't seem terrifically surprised, but I could tell she was hurt.

In the evening, I called Mom and talked to Emily; and then, while Ttina was in the shower, I walked down to the roller coaster and watched the sun drop behind the ocean. The sunsets are unbelievable out here; with big streaks of red and purple and orange painted across the sky. I'm sure I'll never forget it, and I don't see how anyone could ever get used to it.

When it got dark, Mark took us out to dinner and gave me a brand new boogie board. I rode them when I was a kid, and I guess I must have mentioned that in passing. Anyway, I love it, and what better excuse to go jump in the water.

He dropped us off a little later, and then Ttina gave me her present - a botched threesome.

This is sort of how it's been for the last three months: I hang out with Mark and get inspired to push beyond my current situation. Then I come home, and Ttina and I chase a sexual wild goose to the same place we always end up. It always starts out fun, sometimes even euphoric, but if it has been one of those nights, I'll usually wind up exhausted and ashamed and wondering what in the hell just happened.

This time we drank and smoked dope with her friend Dani until well after midnight. I could tell where things were heading, and that wasn't bothering me at all. The music was playing, the tension was building, and there was probably nowhere in the world I would rather have been at that moment. Then, around two, the girls started making out. It was kind of playful at first. They were laughing and talking dirty in a silly way, and I sort of thought they had forgotten about me until Ttina walked over, undid my shorts, and started blowing me.

At this point, I should probably confess that I have always chickened out of anything that ever smelled like a two girl/one guy threesome. This - as opposed to the thing where a willing female agrees to sleep with you and your friend in separate shifts - always seemed like too much pressure. Kind of like playing quarterback in the Super Bowl; a thrilling prospect in the abstract, and who wouldn't want to be at the center of that kind of attention, but you'd sure hate to drop the ball in front of all those people.

I was excited, though, and really enjoying the fellatio performance part of the evening, when Ttina stopped abruptly and looked up at me. She seemed a little woozy, and wanted to move the party into the bedroom. That sounded fine to me, so Dani and I followed her through the doorway and watched as she peeled off into the bathroom.

Unsure of what to do next, I sat on the edge of the mattress and basically waited for the boss to return. It seemed like Dani wanted to proceed, but I was afraid that anything that happened while Ttina was out of the room could technically still be considered cheating - and I had no intention of risking that nightmare.

Dani, however, wasn't worried about that at all. She came in close, stood right in front of me, and lifted up her dress. She had nothing on underneath, and no qualms about it.

"Do you want to get started without her?," she said.

My stomach was a garden of butterflies, and I could feel the warmth of her skin on my face. "We better not," I begged. And then, without asking for permission, she took her dress all the way off and stood there smiling in her birthday suit.

This was Olympic level provocation; and I was stoned, and always very bad at delaying gratification. Still, I was clear headed enough to know that an effort, however insincere, absolutely had to be made to get out of this situation. So I stood up, faked like I was going to walk out of the room, and let her pull my shorts down.

Now I was totally playing with fire, because no ground rules had been set, and Ttina hadn't formally agreed to anything. I really wanted to stop, but I couldn't do it on my own, and Dani wasn't making it any easier. She moved toward me, getting close enough to just barely graze my skin. I took a deep breath, glanced at the bathroom door, then slid my hands from her shoulders to the small of her back. It was pretty much on at this point, and we were just about to kiss, when, from behind the bathroom door, came the unmistakable sound of projectile vomiting.

I guess I got a little carried away and forgot to monitor Ttina's drinking.

And now the sun is up, my teens are over, and I'm lying here naked and nauseous with my partners in the ménage a' trois that wasn't, wondering if this is the best it will ever get without making a fairly big change.

Don't get me wrong, I love Ttina, but our situation gets weirder every time I turn around. As a matter of fact, I don't even have to turn around anymore; all I have to do is walk through the front door, which no longer shuts all the way because I broke it down a couple of weeks ago when Dylan came out from Arizona. Ttina and I got into a fight while we were drinking, then she ran off plastered and naked in the rain. She had a blanket around her, but that didn't stop the cars on Mission Boulevard from screeching to a halt.

I have been learning – and relearning – that there is no good move you can make in a situation like this. You can beg her to get in the truck and talk it over (which I was doing), but that's probably only going to make a drunk girl in a blanket walk faster and scream louder (which she was doing). Sometimes it's better to surrender the battle and hope you can win the war a few beats later; so I decided to drive up to P.B. and turn around, theorizing that the ensuing minute and a half might help her to realize that stomping around in the rain in your bed's clothes isn't as much fun without an audience.

However, when I returned, she was gone. I parked the car and ran back toward the boulevard, looking for her on side streets and in yards, but after about fifteen minutes of searching, I couldn't find her. Then, with nowhere else to turn, I rushed home to call the police.

The rain was still coming down in buckets when I jogged up the exposed staircase that led to our apartment. And when I reached the landing and found the door bolted, I freaked. Dylan was inside, and I couldn't think of a reason why he would lock himself in, so I assumed the worst, and broke the door down. Ttina and I kept fighting, and I kept accusing, until we shut ourselves in the bedroom and started having sex.

This kind of episode doesn't make anyone proud, and it certainly puts a damper on your ability to entertain guests, but that's sort of the way it goes.

And it never seems to get any better; at least not for any length of time. Every crisis is answered with a ramping up of our sexual proclivities. She quits her job, and I fuck her while she's on the phone with her friend. She gets fired, and I fuck her while she's on the phone with some random weirdo from the singles ads. I try to leave, and wind up fucking her in the ass instead. There is constant talk of threesomes and orgies, and there is porno and vibrators and showers in front of her friends, who, by the way, always seem to be sleeping in our bed with us. All of this stuff used to be exciting, but now I'm wondering if maybe neither of us even knows what love is.

Like I heard this story once about Yngwie Malmsteen, the world's fastest guitar player. He was apparently working with a new producer who was trying to broaden his sound. The tape was rolling on an early take, and Yngwie comes ripping out of the gates like a missile. He wants to make a good impression, so he's playing like a runaway train going straight down Mount Everest. The producer listens for a minute, then stops him. Yngwie is confused. He thinks he is doing great, and who on Planet Earth could possibly have played it faster?

The producer says, "Yngwie, give us a little more feeling on this one."

Yngwie thinks he's nuts, but he shrugs and says, Okay.

The tape rolls again, and this time Yngwie really cuts loose, going even faster than the last time. He's about to set the fretboard on fire when the producer cuts him off.

"Yngwie, bro," he says, "we need more feeling."

Bound and determined to deliver more feeling, and getting a little pissed off, Yngwie waits for tape to roll and this time plays so fast you can't even see his fingers. And so on, and so on, and so on...

When I heard this story, I thought, That's me and Ttina. Every time we want more love and security, we answer it with a frantic whoosh past some new – to us - corner of sex. Either that, or a massive catastrophe involving other people, alcohol, or the law. I guess it's what any other addict does when they face resistance or feel a lack; and like all of those other lost souls, it's why Ttina and I have nothing - no material possessions, no prospects, no education, and only the flimsiest of grounding for our relationship.

I couldn't accept this before because I had so little going for me back home; but now, in the light of actual possibility, and in the company of people who really are chasing and achieving supposedly impossible dreams, I can see a little clearer. Mark, for all of his eccentricities, would never dream of wasting time with a strip club, or anything, really, that he couldn't at least hope to be proud of some day. And the thing that bothers me about our situation isn't Ttina. She is her own person, with her own demons to slay. It's me.

I stand at the back of the Improv, night after night, and feel genuine inspiration all around me. I'm learning, too, like how to string words together, and where to end a sentence or a thought for maximum effect. I see why performers go over, and why they don't. And I see that none of this happens by accident. Yes, there is such a thing as aptitude and talent and charisma, but elbow grease is a massive part of the equation. I want to do something like that. I want to express myself in a way that's interesting to others, and hopefully make my living in the process. But I am officially not a kid anymore. And there are guys on that stage who are only a year or two older than me; which keeps me wondering, if not now, then when?

Mark and I went to La Jolla the other night. We had pizza and watched a movie. It was fun, but I could tell he wanted to talk to me about something. He's gentle with advice, and usually prefers to illustrate his point by telling you a story about something dumb he's done. But this time he wasn't sneaking up on me. I think he finds my situation intriguing, though I'm sure he also sees that, at best, I am running in place. I've been trying to keep the soap opera on the down low, but I think Mark senses the general tone of things, because when I told him I wanted out with Ttina, he didn't even argue the point. To the contrary, I think unvarnished stories about us are making their way back to him, and I fear he's beginning to step away from me.

I talked to my dad last night, and he said that unless I went to school, only a fluke could save me. I thought Mark would back that up, and to my surprise, he didn't. Instead, he said, "Focus - that's what you need to succeed. So whether it's this, or being a rocket scientist or a painter, you need to clarify what you want to accomplish and be heading in that direction every day of your life."

"And if I don't?" I asked.

"Well, if you don't, you'll still be heading in some direction, won't you."

11

EXODUS

I'm leaving her. I feel terrible about it, but I have to. So this morning, I tried to fix the door, and failed. Then I loaded up the truck, and went back inside and fucked Ttina. When I returned, all of my money had been stolen. I'm not totally sure that she didn't take it, but I couldn't risk another trip down the rabbit hole which that fight and those recriminations would surely bring, so I borrowed a couple hundred bucks from Mark and hit the road. Ttina made the trip with me - She says she is coming back to live with a roommate — and on the I-8, outside of Yuma, she stripped from the waist down to show her pussy to the truckers we passed. She is crazy. We bring out the worst in each other. I obviously have to get the hell away from her. But God in heaven does she turn me on.

12

THE OLD COLLEGE TRY

I'm back at Arizona State now, and piling on classes fast and furious in the hopes of graduating before the train gets any further down the track. I didn't even have to quit The Improv, because there is one directly across the street from me (not a coincidence – I am subletting a comedy condo from the club). I've probably never felt more inspired, and I owe a good chunk of that to the comedians who are my neighbors while they are in town. I watch their shows carefully, and try to talk to them as often as I can; and they tolerate me because I am related to Mark.

As a group, they are fascinating people. Not as happy as you might imagine; but they read, and observe, and the better ones have a unique perspective on the world.

I also pick up shifts at a crumbling wooden shack by the railroad tracks called The Sun Club. It's kind of a cross between an old tree house and the garage where Hannibal Lecter kept his victim's heads, but it's comfortable, visible from my rear window, and I've seen some amazing bands over there.

It is intoxicating to be around so many creative people; and while this may be a byproduct of simply being in college, it isn't really what happens on campus that excites me. Over there, the goal is career training, and the information is theoretical and delineated. But at The Improv and The Sun Club, the lessons are immediate and vital and emotional and real; and the only true drawback is my appearance, because most artists' memories of guys who look like bodybuilders involve getting beaten up in public. Ironically, this is my history too; so I slump my shoulders, and try to be as non-threatening as possible, and that seems to get me by.

All in all, I'd have to say my life is finally going well. Truly. And I'd almost be tempted to call it perfect if it wasn't for the deranged lunatic who terrorizes Ttina at night.

Okay, so I didn't leave her when I had the chance. Or rather, I left her, then she came back, and I let her in. But come on, there's a mad man out there and he's obviously watching us, because he torments her when I leave for work.

I get these calls during my shifts, and I run to the office to take them. It's Ttina, and she's found a note scratched on the door in her shade of lipstick, or she's just come out of the shower and caught someone diving over the hedge around our patio.

I don't know what to do, but I can't ignore a life and death situation; so I charge through the people waiting to see the show, and race across the street to kill the fucker.

But I can never catch the guy. And you know what really gets me, is how cruel and indifferent people can be. Like here lately, I've caught Chuck, the manager of the club, laughing at me. It's as though he thinks she's lying or something. Well you know what, Fuck Chuck. That big, Christian asshole is probably just jealous because my girlfriend is so hot. I mean, how crass to make jokes at a time like this. And why would anyone fake like a maniac was after them?

Still, Chuck's smile isn't a "maybe" grin, it's more of a "You poor bastard," one. So when I get home, I take a hard look around, paying careful attention to what I see. It's mostly the usual stuff: a little wine, a vibrator, a stack of horror books. Then, all of the sudden, something clicks, and I start thinking, Maybe, just maybe, when I'm not here, she gets bored and... She makes shit up!

The more I ponder this, the more it seems like a real possibility. But when I bring it up to her, first she throws a fit, and the next thing I know I'm lying on my back at the Dream Palace with a dollar bill in my teeth, and an unfamiliar vagina heading straight toward my face.

Damn, it seems like I'm here a lot lately.

My friends and I come to the Palace more than I care to admit, but the weird shit happens when I'm with Ttina. Frequently, we wind up in the back room, stoned out of our minds, and alone with some dancer who is looking me dead in the eye as she shows us her pussy. A couple of times these girls have even come home with us, but Ttina and I can never work up the courage to do anything with them.

I guess what I'm saying is; if it was weird before, it's Bizarro Land now, and I'm afraid if this continues, one of us is going to end up in jail or the sanitarium.

But it does continue – and continue, and continue - until one morning, shortly after the phantom stalker drops us from his rounds, something inside of me breaks, and the whole demented thing just ends.

Ttina is working at a restaurant that does a Sunday brunch. Their doors open early, and she has to be there by six a.m. sharp. This is a new job, and I work late, and how much trouble can you really get into at that hour? So I loan her my truck – because I guess I'll never learn – and off she goes as dawn is breaking.

At around ten, I roll out of bed and open the curtains, and as I do, my truck rolls right by me. Ttina is in the passenger seat, and a guy in a waiter's uniform is driving. They pass quickly, and continue on to the back of the building, even though our parking spot is right in front of the sliding glass door.

It's clear now that something big is about to occur, so I brace myself, and wait in a state of suspended animation until someone begins fumbling with the deadbolt. This continues long enough for five people to have unlocked and relocked the door, and then Ttina enters. She is shitfaced (apparently, it's a champagne brunch they serve over there), and hitting me with a glare that indicates that she is not home early to request absolution. No, she clearly intends to go with the old stand-by; an attempt to pin her crimes on me before a jury of me. Which, frankly, is a bit of a relief, because she only ever tries this when she is too drunk to pull it off.

183

I cross my arms, and away she goes, like the world's worst magician, clumsily stuffing a frightened rabbit into a hat in front of the very audience she means to fool. It is a pathetic performance, and she knows it, which can only mean one thing: Violence is on its way.

Her rage builds. Then, with motor skills drowning in sparkling wine, she takes a slow-motion wind up, and stumbles toward me throwing a big, sloppy haymaker. It's so obvious I want to laugh, but instead I lean back to dodge her fist, then step forward, throwing a quick punch of my own. This is pure reflex, and my sheer stupidity and lack of self control register at exactly the same moment that my knuckles connect with the back of her skull.

My whole moral code flashes before my eyes. This was not self defense, and I did not need to hit anyone. I could very easily have wrapped her up and endured the screaming until the cops came. I've certainly done that before. But instead, I'm looking at the back of her head as she pushes up off the couch and thinking, "Oh my God, that felt good!" Followed by, "Holy shit, I just punched a girl," then a quick burst of, "Maybe I can control this situation through violence," before finally settling on, "I have to dump this nut and get a place of my own – today."

And so I do. Then two months later I quit The Improv and go back to work in another topless bar.

PART FOUR

ON TO

WASHINGTON

(With a Few More Hours in California)

1

THE DEEP END

"Why don't you get married."

"Huh…" Mom is speaking, but, to be honest, her boobs are hogging all of my attention.

"I just think maybe if you get married, you will feel better."

Boobs, boobs, boobs… She's forty-four years old; how on earth did she grow giant boobs overnight?

"Sweetie, are you listening to me?"

"Um, yeah… Did you get another boob job?"

She smiles. I've noticed. And how could anyone help but notice; she's wearing a bikini, and she hasn't stopped rubbing baby oil into her chest since Emily and I walked through the door. "It's a breast lift, sweetie. And yes, I had a couple of procedures performed."

I look closer; her face seems tighter, and her lips are fatter than usual. "Um… Okay." I guess I should come over more often – or maybe never come back here again.

"Can I go swimming, Mommy?," says Emily.

"Yes, sweetie, but put on your bathing suit first."

"Okay," she says, and scampers off to her room to change. We've been at the movies today, and I'm sort of in a rush to get going before Ray comes home because the tension over here is at an all time high. Which is one of the reasons I'm surprised to hear Mom suggesting marriage as a remedy for the depression I've been feeling since Ttina and I split up.

"So are you going to?" she asks.

"Get married?"

"Sure, why not, as long as it isn't one of those strippers, like Ttina. Those girls are so trashy," she says, rubbing another handful of oil into her bosom.

"Yeah, well, I'll give it some thought; but we only broke up a month ago, and I'm not even dating anyone."

"I'm just saying," sayeth Mom, as she snaps the cap on the oil, and stashes it under her patio chair.

"Watch, Mommy!" Emily has returned - in water wings and a little kid's one piece - and she wants an audience for the cannonball she is about to execute in the shallow end.

"Okay, love, let's see," Mom smiles and puts her giant circle sunglasses on as Emily faces the pool in preparation for her dive. "Look out, Craigy, I don't want to get you wet."

I am way out of the splash zone for a forty-pound girl, but to boost her confidence, I push back and cover my head with my hands. She giggles, which gives me enough time before the dive proper, to see a pattern of small red welts on the top of her legs.

"Does Emily have a rash?" I ask, as she leaps into the water, creating barely a ripple.

Mom cuts off the questioning with an abrupt and scowling, "No," then beams again as Emily surfaces. "That was wonderful, sweetie! The biggest splash ever."

"Did you like it, Craigy?"

"Yeah," I smile, "nice job, Petunia."

"Tell me if this one's bigger, okay?"

"Will do," I nod, and then turn back to Mom.

"Look, I don't want to get into it right now," Mom announces before I even have a chance to follow up. And because this kind of proclamation never made anyone less curious, I repeat, this time verbally, "If she doesn't have a rash, then what are those red marks on her legs?"

Mom narrows her eyes, as she does when anything dares puncture her glamorous, angel of mercy, super mom delusion, and says, "He hits her with a brush."

My jaw drops, and I am about to tee off when Emily surfaces from her most recent cannonball. "How was that one!"

"That was great," I respond; and she says, "Okay, I'm going to the deep end. Watch me!"

Putting on about the worst fake smile imaginable, I nod; and as she begins inching her way, hand over hand, around the edge of the tiny pool, I turn to Mom and whisper, "Are you fucking kidding me? He's hitting her with a brush, and you're just letting that happen?"

"Oh, she doesn't even listen to him anymore. She just thinks he's a big joke."

"She thinks her two hundred and fifty pound father is a joke!," I stammer. And suddenly, I want to grab Emily and

189

run for the hills, because I know exactly what's driving this. First, Ray is a shaky, immature, and volatile dude. Second, he has too big an ego to acknowledge the many games that are being played on him. And third, and more specifically, I've been watching this shit build for most of the past year and a half.

Back then, Ttina and I were broke, about to lose the apartment, and between jobs. We had nothing to eat, and I asked Mom for a loan. She refused, but stopped by later with a bag containing everything stale in her cupboard or about to go bad in her fridge. It was like three slimy hot dogs, a half full jar of olives, some old peanut butter, and an open sleeve of rubbery crackers, all passed to me with the hushed admonition not to tell Ray. Which might still have been welcome, if she hadn't also brought Emily and her new "friend," Eric, along as witnesses.

This guy was an electro douche insurance salesman with artistic pretensions, and I hated him right off the bat. He wasn't unusual in any way; he had weak eyes and an even weaker, though beard enhanced, chin. And like all of the other middle aged Romeos who preceded him, he arrived with the annoying conviction that he was flying in under my radar. But that was to be expected. It was more that Emily was with them that made me want to grab Mom and her new buddy by the neck, and march them back to her shitass convertible and set it on fire. This, however, would not be necessary, because the first thing she said after handing me her sack of trash was that she couldn't stay because she was going to Eric's house to pose for him.

As usual, she was multi-tasking. Demonstrating her amazing motherliness to the new stooge, while putting me in my place by handing me some token charity, and forcing a secret on me that I did not want to share, but now had to. The most galling part, though – and likely the chief reason for the visit – was that she was getting my tacit sign off on the "friendship" for Emily, whose own feelings of creepiness she was clearly hoping to muddle. Of course, there was also a larger message intended for everyone present, including Ttina. It was the core theme of her life: a narcissistic declaration of beauty, compassion and sexual attractiveness meant for everyone, but particularly her husbands and lovers and children. She would never articulate her message (because a verbal statement can be analyzed and refuted), preferring instead to perform it like a piece of abductive, interactive, interpretive dance. But the basic idea was, "I am the merciful center of charity, elegance, and grace; and so many men want to fuck me, I can hardly keep track of them all (though I am not to blame for their lusty attentions), Amen."

This was nothing new, and I'd been rolled up in her spider web enough that I was sort of used to it. However, I'd never seen her drag a strange guy in front of Emily before. And because I'd been down this road so many times, I knew where it was heading, how it would get there, and who it would hurt the most.

The affair would only be fun if Ray found out – or at least wondered if it was happening. Therefore, when she brought home the laughably amateurish product of her afternoon of modeling - an orange and yellow striped portrait of herself in an unbuttoned man's shirt, which just barely covered her nipples – my guess is she offered it to Ray as a gift. He, like any other man, wouldn't have wanted it, so she would then play hurt, thereby making him feel guilty for her prelude to infidelity. Now, instead of hanging on the wall, the painting would be (and was) stuck in the closet, so that it would be visible to Ray every time the door was opened. In Mom to human speak, this ploy says, "You have hurt me by not accepting my gift, and you are also petty and insecure for refusing to believe that I love you, and you alone." And, "However, you should also be aware that I am a glamorous artist's model, and if you do not shower me with jealous and desperate attention, some day I may be in love with this painter, or some other mysterious, artistic type."

Of course, this nonsense keeps the marriage heading in the wrong direction, which causes Mom to shore up her only ally, Emily, by portraying anything Ray does that feels even remotely like discipline, as unreasonable and abusive. Soon Emily is looking to Mom to find out if she has to obey whatever order her father is giving her; then Ray, feeling undercut by a woman old enough to be his mother, becomes enraged, leading to either a blow up, or a piling on of more suppressed fury. And the whole dance begins anew at the next level of severity.

This dynamic was all too familiar to me, and Mary would also have easily spotted it if she'd been around. But what was particularly galling, was that Mom was still content to let a four year-old suffer the blowback from her manipulations; just as I'd endured Dad's wrath when I was Emily's age (and Ray's later on). And the most confusing part for the child caught in the middle is, after you have taken your ass-kicking, or worse, she moves in with an extremely seductive message of, "It's so horrible what that man does to us, but we'll get through this because it's me and you against the world," which cuts you off from one parent, and makes you feel guilty for not being able to protect the other from the abuse that she has provoked and you've just endured.

It is a deeply confusing cycle of manipulation, which has the ironic effect of making you believe that she is your best and only friend. You may catch on in glimpses, but she'll never admit a thing. And if you question her methods or motives, she will act hurt and probably bring on the tears. Then your internal compass will go to shit, because your heart knows that something is wrong, but allowing your brain to believe it seems like the ultimate betrayal. Suddenly north is not north – it is whatever she wants you to believe it is - and your own intuitive sense of the wrongness of things can only be processed as disloyal, paranoid suspicion.

And this I fear for Emily more than any physical abuse that some man of our mother's might bring; that she will feel the storm, but never be allowed to acknowledge it. That she will be cut off from people with clearer perspective, and made suspicious of them when they get too close. And that the blame for Mom's trail of destruction will be assigned to a defenseless little girl who has been made to worship her, even as the infallible Madonna stands in the eye of the twister, grinding her weather machine, with no sincere concern for anything except that which bolsters and affirms her wildly inflated self image.

And back at the pool, I literally want to puke as Mom continues to encourage Emily on her trek toward the deep end. It's hard for adults to understand this shit, even if they've lived through it, and a little girl has no chance at all. So I make one last attempt to appeal to her sense of decency by saying, "Mom, you need to protect your children from the men in your life." And for a second, I let her bog me down in the phrase, "...the men in your life."

"I have not been promiscuous!" She exclaims. Then I bring up the gym guy, the dentist guy, the aluminum foil guy, and the guys from Dad's office. And when I wrap back around to the pool guy who was our first up close Eric, she defiantly proclaims, "It was the seventies!"

I'm done. There is no talking to this person, and I am scared to death for my little sister. I get up to kiss Emily good-bye, and Mom gives me her pitiable look and says, "My father was inappropriate too, you know." And if this is true, it is horrible, but I feel no sympathy for her at all. A little girl, sure, of course. But thirty years on, if you're not looking out for your own kids, then you may even be worse than your victimizer because you know how it feels.

It is horrible, and I don't know what to do about Emily, but I do know that I can't take this anymore. I can't take Mom anymore. Back in the day, I tried to talk to her about the fingers up the ass, and ball grabbing, and all of the other shit I was living with during her marital reconciliation in Florida; and not only did she deny that it ever happened, she spent the next three years telling me that if it wasn't for me and my behavior, she could still be living in a beautiful house by the beach instead of a shitty apartment in Oklahoma. And I believed that, right up to the day I confessed to Mark back in San Diego that I had destroyed my parents' marriage. He laughed, thinking I was kidding, and then, when he realized that I was serious, he looked me in the eye and said, "You know that's not possible. If anything, you might have given them a project to work on which kept them together for longer."

And thank God I have that to lean on now, because as I kiss Emily, and she begs me to stay and witness more amazing feats of swimming and diving, I need every ounce of strength I can muster to overcome the guilt and impotence I feel over not being able to help her. I have to get out of here. This isn't funny anymore, and understanding my mother only makes me more confused about what to do, and whom to trust, and even what is real in the world and what is a mirage. I do know, however, that I have to do something for Emily - if I can.

2

BACK TO THE FUTURE

I'd be lying if I said I didn't have a prurient reason for going back to work at a strip club. And it would be disingenuous to pretend like compulsion or compassion, or the behavior of anyone else drove me back here, when the simple truth is that after a couple of months without Ttina, I was lonely, and normal girls with families, and friends, and boundaries just didn't do it for me. I mean, with emotional health and support systems like that, what would my job be anyway?

I did try, though. I moved in with a guy from the Improv, and planned to only date girls from school or the gym. I even went out with another virgin for a while. She was seeing me and a coke dealer – and if you add that to her virginity, you probably get a psychology more complex than Ttina's and mine put together.

This was a frustrating few weeks which earned me a prize winning set of blue balls, and a conversation with a female friend who told me that some girls do everything but intercourse, and never intend to go any further until marriage. I'd never encountered that particular cat in the jungle before, but I'd already seen enough of civilian females, so I decided to return to what was familiar.

I did not, however, come back with my tail between my legs. I could have worked almost anywhere I wanted to. I have lots of friends in the nightclub business, and getting door jobs is not difficult. And I'm also not sad that I can't get on with normal girls because they bore me to tears. Where is the harrowing backstory? And what about the crazy sexual past for me to obsess over? I mean, don't you at least have an unsolvable personality disorder for me to work on, because I've got time on my hands and I need to do some rescuing.

At some point, I think you just have to be honest with yourself about your own level of freakiness. I mean, do you want to watch Andy Griffith or *The Last Picture Show*? Do you want to hear Pat Boone or Little Richard? And do you want to go on a bunch of dates and have respectable missionary intercourse with a girl who isn't emotionally dependent on you, or would you rather have desperate, pathological, "What In The Fuck Is Wrong With Us?" sex with a professional titillater at all hours of the day and night? I have sincerely enjoyed both sides of these equations (except for Pat Boone), I just happen to like one more than the other – in a very, very big way.

I am also aware that topless bars, and the boys and girls, and men and women who work in them are frowned upon. Believe me, people yell all kinds of shit when they drive past the club at night. But all they're really saying is, "I'm so fucking curious about what goes on in there, and damn-it am I hard up and jealous!" Otherwise, why not cruise past in silent disapproval; and why even bother to notice us at all? Really, fuck them if they don't like this place—that only makes me like it more.

I enjoy being an outcast. There is nowhere to fall from outcast, and nothing to pretend. At least here at Candy's, Scottsdale's Finest Cabaret, no one can put on airs – even though cabaret is the most ridiculous aggrandizement of titty bar in the history of man. So it's sleazy - fine. So I'm sleazy - even more fine. I'm in college now, and someday I'll move on, but at the moment, I like it here. I like the girls, and I like the DJs, and the cocktail waitresses, and the loud rock'n'roll. (Though I would happily beat everyone in Poison to death with the severed limbs of the members of Warrant.) I even like the club itself. It's small, and there is a big, wooden horseshoe stage in the center, which sort of underscores the performance aspect of stripping.

And one more thing: Maybe its an intuitive thing, or perhaps it's a commonality of background, and it might even be that I am body conscious and so are most dancers; but strippers have liked me from day one, and I have liked them right back. Simple as that. And I may get a little down on myself once in a while, but I know who I am, and I know what I'm into, and at this stage of the game, most of the resistance I get comes from people I have no interest in anyway. I turned twenty-one a month ago. I am an adult. And there is something inside of me that's drawn to a certain kind of place and a certain kind of person; and at the moment, I am willing to live with that.

3

RAY

I am twenty-one and my mother's husband is twenty-nine. He used to bully me, but things have changed. We are about the same size now, but I am stronger and I look one hell of a lot better; which I can say with full humility because I put more into this than he does.

In fairness, though, I owe a lot to Ray. He got me started working out. Six years ago, on my fifteenth birthday, he drove me to the only gym I had ever used and showed me what to do. Then, during that first month, he made sure I ate enough to gain the weight I wanted to put on. In the time since, there isn't much positive to discuss, but I do owe him an acknowledgement of that much.

Now I am on my own, though, and as I've said, things are different. The change started after I won my first contest; which earned me some respect from Ray, and dramatically advanced my standing in the gym. Laugh if you must, but winning a show gives you a name, literally;

like, "That guy is Mr. Phoenix," or, "Joe is Mr. Tucson." Perhaps obviously, then, the best you can do in this state is Mr. Arizona. If you bring home that trophy, then every serious guy in every gym in the big population centers will know your name. And while I am too young to even place in that show, I did do the next best thing – at least for a nineteen year-old.

I won the Teenage Arizona while being trained, free of charge, by my good friend and neighbor, Hank, who was, you guessed it, Mr. Arizona. And it gets better; Hank's best friend was a professional bodybuilder named Vinnie, who helped me out too. Almost before I knew it, I had a community of very intimidating friends, which included nearly every heavy hitter who came into the gym (where I worked, briefly). It was like that line in "Little Deuce Coupe" that goes, "All the bad guys know us and they leave us alone." Well, Dylan and I know all the bad guys, and we get left alone.

And now, a couple of years on, Ray has taken an interest in me that can feel like admiration, and sometimes envy. It's not a permanent state; it comes and goes. And I wouldn't say that we are friends either, just occasionally friendly. It's like sometimes he looks at me and sees a guy who goes to college (He did not.), has pretty girlfriends, and is at the top of the social heap in one of the main bodybuilding gyms in the Valley; and other times he sees the same person and thinks, "Who in the fuck does that punk think he is?" I'm sure that being married to my mother doesn't help, particularly during the current decline, which anyone with a pair of eyeballs could have seen coming a mile away. It's a strange situation, and sometimes

I wonder if I am part of his bail out strategy, or just on his murder/suicide checklist.

Anyway, now he wants to work out at my gym on his way home from work. He has even asked a few times if I would go with him; so I have. We don't train together often, but he is becoming a semi-regular over here, which in a lot of ways underscores our strange reversal of positions. He asks me about diet, routine, and even drugs (though I don't think he takes them); and I've introduced him to some of my friends who compete, many of whom are his age or older; including my roommates, Thad, who is thirty-two and studying to be a doctor, and Jerry, who is thirty-four and recently divorced.

At this gym, Ray is just a face in the crowd, and he doesn't really fit in. It's near the college, so most everyone is either a young student or a serious bodybuilder or power lifter, and he is neither. But he is with me now, and that is odd – to look across the room and see this person who was once my tormentor, and have a quasi-paternal feeling of, "I hope the guys are nice to him." And they are, which is good. I've even caught myself wondering if maybe this new state of affairs will help cool the tension surrounding Emily; although the eight hundred pound gorilla in that situation is my mom - and with the boob job and puffy lip injections she is probably more like eight hundred and five pounds.

4

THE LAY OF THE LAND

I get to work at six and park my motorcycle behind the Dunkin' Donuts, near the club's office. It is one shitty room - the business hub of Candy's - in a row of about five shitty rooms that back up to a mall-sized vacant lot full of Palos Verdes bushes and trash. There's a few old cars back there, and an even older carpet cleaning wagon, and none of this is visible from the road; which is the drawing card for me. My bike is a piece of junk, but I want to keep it, and this beats the hell out of the unlit gravel lot behind the bar, where anything goes.

Edie, by way of contrast, is our star attraction. She gets to work whenever she pleases, and parks her brand new convertible at the front door. It is a Mustang; big and white, like her hair.

At the beginning of my shift, the sun is still scorching the tiny pink erection where I work. It's a pretentious building which looks sort of like a monastery; though all you have to do is open the door to know that Candy's is no place for worship or solitude.

I arrive at happy hour, so the room is festive and the song is something like *Hard to Handle*, *Paradise City* or *Sexy, Mexican Maid*; though there is dance stuff too - *Unbelievable* and *Groove is in the Heart* jump to mind, and usually don't leave until I've had a few days off. The rest of the night will be rowdy, or at least obsessive and drunk, but these first couple of hours are different; more social, because until around eight, Candy's is basically a neighborhood joint.

Meanwhile, in a fancy apartment across town, Edie is deciding where to have dinner, and whether or not she will work this evening. Todd, her live-in boyfriend, is a DJ on a Phoenix rock station, so if there's a concert, we probably won't see her. And if she does decide to come in, it may be an hour or two past sundown before she makes her entrance.

We will be waiting.

Back here, in the vestibule of Candy's, my sight has returned, so I round the corner into the main room and head toward the regulars at the bar. They're usually clogging the lane by the mini stage, and I'm usually beating back lines from songs like *Piano Man* and *Main Street* as I squeeze past, saying my hellos. This moment always feels the same for me; kind of like passing through a black velvet painting of sad clowns, cigarettes, burlesque floozies, and bottles of booze.

In real life, though, these guys are a disparate bunch, similar only in their desire to be here as the sun sets. Some of them – the sleazy, coked-up, middle-aged low-lifes - are friends of Wayne's, the guy who owns the place. They are predictable to the point of stereotypical, standing by the wall trying to get the girls to go out with them, or pose for the "gentleman's magazine" that they are always loudly conspiring to start. These men are garden variety scumbags, and thankfully they never stay long because being in Wayne's circle of skuzzy, drunken, tweaker dudes is the whole point of their existence, and no one wants to overstay their welcome.

The rest of the happy hour crew is cool enough. There's a few businessmen, some construction workers, a biker named J.D. whose girlfriend dances the day shift, and a pair of alcoholic codgers working dueling shticks for the girls. One is short, early seventies, and screams "Whoooaah!" when they take the stage or remove their tops, and the other is a crapulous Frankenstein who lurks at the bar folding dollar bills into wedding rings, which he puts on the dancers' fingers as tips. You certainly wouldn't want either of these degenerates as, say, a Thanksgiving guest, but if I had to choose one, the "Whoooaah!" guy wins hands down because he is, at least, happy, whereas the Wedding Ring Frankenstein is a total goon.

At the end of the bar, a glass wall hides the service well and time clock. I arrive during the shift change for dancers, so I'm usually punching in with the night girls as the day girls clock out. Trash cans and server traffic keep anyone from lingering here for too long, but as I pass the restrooms and the DJ booth (where I say a quick "hey" to Ritchie, the fifty year-old voice of Candy's), the cold war radiating from the dressing room is palpable. The issue is shiftism – specifically, the night girls looking down upon the day girls. And because the door is always open, I have seen many a silent (and occasionally, not so silent) battle unfold. Imagine the popular girls and the nerdy ones in the gym class locker room, or the opening act and the headliner at a rock show. It's probably not nice to say, but it is also totally obvious, the day girls are the B team, and the night girls are the varsity; and unless someone is being punished, or we are super short handed, never the twain shall meet (except during the changing of the guard).

The dancers on the day shift at Candy's (and everywhere else) are... earthier, and usually shaped differently than the hoofers of the night – who are all either beautiful, sexy, young, unusual in an interesting way, or some almost good enough combination of these qualities attached to a big personality. The day girls aren't ugly, though; just kind of like the female patrons of a bowling alley – only naked. Some are cute, some are druggy, some are older, and some are nasty (meaning, it's them you have to keep an eye on, not the guys they're dancing for). And there are still others, like J.D.'s girl, who seem to have had hard lives, and just want to get the day over with so they can go home and be with their man.

It's probably fair to say that most nighttime dancers want to be movie stars and supermodels, and while none are actually pursuing these goals in any meaningful way, a healthy percentage have nude photos taken by some semi-professional someone tucked away in shoeboxes or heavy envelopes. Their age range is roughly eighteen to twenty-four, give or take a few years for fake I.D.'s and older women sliding backward into the dayshift minor leagues. They go to clubs, they party, they buy expensive clothes, and love to be recognized for their sexiness. And with regard to money; they generate a lot, spend even more, and are usually in a big rush to make rent toward the end of any given month. I'd say about two thirds are regular employees, with the odd third filled out by rolling stoners from the Phoenix stripper circuit, mystery women from out of town, and new girls getting started in the business.

Of course, Edie is no exception to any of this. Rather, just as a broad characterization of reggae musicians might also describe Bob Marley, this depiction of night shift dancers is a foundational, but not all inclusive, introduction to Edie – whom Troy and I are waiting for outside the club, now that it is nine and the night has officially begun to hum.

Troy, my best friend on the staff, is a twenty-three year-old, movies and music obsessed, ex-Marine with an Elvis haircut and a sly sense of humor. He is an anomaly among the bouncers I have known (and the Marines, for that matter); first, because he has absolutely no desire to tell anyone what to do; and second, although he is tall and skinny, never works out, eats like shit, and chain smokes, people still listen to him when he tells them that it's time to go. He is bright too, but has no plans to go to college or better himself in any way. As a matter of fact, if I came back in twenty years I'll bet he'd be managing the place, which is sad, because with a little confidence, Troy could probably be anything he wanted to be. (And I usually think, actor in a war movie who gets killed in the fifth reel, or Mickey Rourke's friend in something.)

Troy's sister, Charlene, works here too. She is an unmarried, pregnant cocktail waitress, who is also funny.

Troy told me once that their dad (abandoning, like everyone else's in here) was a country musician in the upper Midwest, and I'll bet that's where they get their charm — though again, I've never met two more capable people who were less convinced of their own capabilities.

If it's slow, Troy and I will spend a big chunk of the night outside talking. We card the guys who approach the door, greet the usual suspects, and probably answer about ten questions per evening from dirtheads, other dancers, and the manager concerning Edie's whereabouts. It can get a little tedious, but it's usually fun, just hanging around shooting the bull. And often our friends will see us as they drive past, and stop to chat; which provides them with an excuse to go inside. I know Wayne would prefer us to be indoors all night, but spending eight hours inside of a smoky topless bar without coming up for air can be suffocating, especially when so many of your own gender are behaving so poorly. And besides, if someone is being a jerk, one of the girls will come and get us.

On the weekends, or during fraternity or bachelor parties, the mood can change abruptly. One minute everyone is relaxed, Ritchie's telling jokes on the mic, and we're all sort of bullshitting the night away; and then, from out of nowhere, a bunch of rowdy drunks barge in and demand to be entertained. And as with any place that combines alcohol and sexual frustration, there will be fights and combative assholes; which means eventually you will have to break something up, or toss someone out. But that doesn't happen too often, and on most nights this is a pretty good job.

Edie makes it better, though. And when she gets here, even the girls that don't like her – and they are legion – step up their game; not because she is the boss, but because she is the center of gravity.

Edie is the front man of the rock band that is Candy's. She struts, she preens, and she plays the crowd the way Eddie Van Halen works a guitar. And like Eddie, if you stood and watched her do the thing she's great at – exuding sex appeal – you might be tempted to assign all kinds of other, wonderful qualities to her as well. Like, "Man, Edie is hot, I'll bet she's a genius." And in a way, even that is true, because Edie instinctively knows what my marketing professors have dedicated their lives to understanding – simplicity is the best message, and sex sells.

Edie is also off the charts vain and egotistical; which, of course, only makes her more appealing. She knows what she is and refuses to shy away from it, and for this reason, she reminds me of an NBA center wearing KISS boots to look taller, or maybe Sasquatch in a fur coat. She is a bully of beauty, and where most hot girls will wear less revealing costumes on the floor, she makes a point of wearing the most revealing. There are probably a million things you could say about an attractive person's appeal without ever hitting the nail exactly on the head, but one of the best ways to capture Edie might be through the music she plays on stage.

Edie is very particular about what gets played and when, and only she is allowed to play her songs when she is working. She owns all kinds of power ballads, industrial music, mood stuff, and metal; but the three tracks I hear her play most are: *Epic* by Faith No More, with the chorus that goes, "You want it all, but you can't have it!," which she interprets self-referentially. *Edie* by The Cult, for obvious reasons. And, most astoundingly, the militant race anthem, *Am I Black Enough For Ya?* by Schoolly D – and she is a five foot, two inch blonde girl! Even if you hate her, it's hard not to have at least some grudging respect for the sheer nerve of a person like Edie. I certainly do. However, I keep that to myself, because everyone in this room has a crush on her, probably even the girls who can't stand her. She is not smart, or kind, or generous, but she has rock star charisma, and a total belief in her own beauty, and that kind of self absorption tends to suck up everything in its path.

5

THE FOG

It always comes back, no matter how far away I get. Months will go by, sometimes nearly a year, and I'll start to believe that those were the bad old days, and that age and experience have finally taught me how to manage my emotions. I'll remind myself of the tools I've collected along the way, and how effective they can be when applied with a strong, Schwarzneggerian will. I go to the gym, avoid drugs and alcohol, and steer clear of my mother. I'll make sure to eat right, study hard, stay busy, and seek out friends. Sometimes I'll begin a new project, or go climb the mountain, which can be extremely helpful in getting things in perspective. And if there is a new job to start or girl to date, then so much the better.

But no matter how good, or even manageably bad, things are, eventually the clouds will return. This usually happens very gradually, and then all at once. Like I'll be walking home from school and realize that I'm talking to myself in my father's voice again, real critical and insistent. I know what this means, and I don't take it lightly. I'll make every attempt to ignore him, and I'll get to work on other things. The grades will come up, the muscles will get bigger, and the money will increase because I'm taking on more hours and sleeping less. Inevitably, though, the dread accelerates and the haze gets thicker. So I pile on more shit, and reach for Arnold's example as a model of what can realistically be achieved. The diet will get strict, and I might even start feeling religious, or more aware of God and what He wants from me. Somewhere in here, I'll start to notice that I'm spending a lot of time alone. I'm still going to the gym everyday, but I'm not meeting up with Dylan, and I'm keeping my distance even from the good people I know.

Then the cloud descends, and I begin living my life in it. It's just sadness, really – but a totally overbearing, irrational, and all encompassing sadness. I will still be doing the normal stuff - going to work, school, etc. - but I'm also getting more irritable and prickly. I'm probably crying a lot too, and skipping classes. My grades drop, I lose my temper, and the world starts to seem black and hopeless. Eventually, I will bog down in the sensation that I am invisible and living in a bubble, and I'll find myself staring deep into my own eyes, as if it were possible to find and remove the source of the sadness. Sex is unpredictable during these periods, but never on an even keel. I'll either have no interest, or be wanting to fuck all of the time. And when the loneliness gets really heavy, I'll wind up at Ttina's depressing studio apartment near the community college, screwing her while she slurs dirty talk at me.

It isn't always bad, though; even during these stretches there are moments in most days when I laugh with my friends, or take a deep breath and realize how beautiful the night is. But the fog is my default setting, and literally a pain in my neck and back.

When the bottom finally drops all the way out, there may be months where just getting my train of thought rolling straight is a chore. Concentration becomes a Herculean endeavor, and an incredibly convincing paranoia sets in. Usually, I know that my mind is playing tricks on me, but sometimes it gets weird enough that I wind up at mom's house, feeling like I have nowhere else to turn, and sobbing uncontrollably. The words are probably a little different each time, but the feeling is exactly the same; total powerlessness, complete defeat, and pure disgust with myself.

And then, with a heart full of "Why in the fuck not, it certainly couldn't get any worse," I'll start drinking. At first it's just hanging out with the guys, or having a few in the bar after the shift. But gradually, I become a pro, throwing back pitchers and shots in the afternoon with Troy, or whomever, until it's time to go to work, or out to chase down more trouble. In a normal job, being hammered on the clock would be a big and noticeable problem, but there really isn't anyone minding the store at Candy's. The girls party in the dressing room, and sometimes we'll be sneaking stuff out of the liquor closet. There's a fair amount of coke floating around too. I dabble, but rarely, if ever, take anything out of the club. Usually, I'm just doing a couple lines with Ritchie in the DJ booth, and then getting back on the job, feeling bright eyed and bushy tailed.

It's nothing serious. And, while I've broken some of my own rules about mixing steroids, alcohol, and narcotics; you know, so what. Life is strange, and sometimes you have to roll with it. It's weird too that I feel better at work. Maybe because misery loves company, or maybe it's simply that there's no place to hide out and brood. I've been in this world long enough that I have relatively old friends in the business. Crystal, the first dancer I ever slept with, works here now, and so does Amy, the girl from Bourbon Street who used to tell me sex stories about her adventures with rock bands. Her mom, Geena, works here too - as a bartender - and I know her pretty well because she went out with Dylan for about a year and a half. And many other familiar faces come and go. So many, in fact, that I probably can't consider myself a tourist anymore. I have become the big guy in Florida with the puffy hair who let me into The Cheetah all those years ago. I don't have nightmares about working at a place like this anymore because the life isn't even peculiar to me. It's just life, and one day I'll leave it; probably when I graduate from college, and hopefully alone, but I'm not sure.

There is this, though; I do not fuck around. There is opportunity to screw girls indiscriminately, but I'm not into that; I promise. I'm not sure why. Stomping across Texas looking for Andie and our baby definitely changed my feelings about casual sex. I'm not saying that I've been perfect since then, but I am saying that I have trended in a particular direction.

And now there is Edie. Perhaps I'm reading too much into this, but here lately she has been asking me to pick up an extra order of Pad Thai when I run across the street to get my dinner. Maybe she just likes Thai food all of the sudden, but I've definitely noticed that when I get back, pretty much every time, she's sitting around naked in the dressing room waiting for me to deliver it to her – and this is not every day behavior for dancers. Topless, sure – that's every day – but walking in on girls hanging out totally nude is like a once a week thing, and it's usually not the same one. But Edie is weird. Who knows what she's up to. She could just be teasing. However, yesterday, when I got back, she stood up and flashed me by bending over with her bare ass facing in my direction. And that's never happened to me before – anywhere, ever. I wonder what she's up to.

6

ONE ENCHANTED EVENING

I just got done fucking Edie. It was so cool, and she is so hot; but it's four thirty in the morning, and she said she'd be back an hour ago. She was going to break up with Todd, which I am totally stoked about. I mean it's all so new, but it just feels so right, you know.

How new? Well, that's a good question. Let's see, if you add the hour I've been waiting, to the hour we were having sex, and combine that with the forty-five minutes her "Dear John" trip was supposed to take, then our romance is just under three hours old. A little fresh, I'll grant you, but she's leaving the guy she lives with after just one night with me, and it doesn't get any realer than that.

I only wish she'd hurry up and get back, because I already miss her. It's crazy. I just feel so happy. If only there was someone I could call at this hour to share the good news, but it's probably too late. Yeah... four thirty is pretty late - definitely too late.

215

Anyway, we were just having breakfast with Troy after work, which I was freaking completely out over because Edie doesn't usually talk to us that much. It was going well, though. No big deal. Then I thought for a minute she was going to leave with another guy who I'd seen around; but when I said I was taking off, she ran right over and we left in her car. Troy went home... Maybe I could call him... No, probably better not.

When we got back here, I was amazed at how quickly things went. We were going to watch TV so I threw a couple of pillows on the ground (so as not to seem too forward) and she jumped right over them and landed on the bed. Five minutes later we were all the way into it.

And now I'm just waiting. They probably have a lot to talk about. It's tough to get news like this, especially in the middle of the night...

Wait a second. I think that's her. Yeah, there's her car. Oh, awesome - I knew she'd come back!

Thank you, God.

7

TWO MONTHS WITH EDIE

So Edie came back, and she was perfectly honest about where she'd been – having sex with Todd. But, you know, break ups are dicey, and we talked it over for a few minutes and went ahead and had sex again. After that, we went to Jack In The Box for a bite to eat, because by then the sun was coming up, and we'd been having all that sex – especially her.

The next couple of weeks were like something from a dream. Well, maybe not two whole weeks. Probably closer to ten days. We decided right off the bat not to live together – I have roommates, and she has no desire to live together - and we moved her into a new place by the club. There was intercourse, lots and lots of intercourse, and we made out everywhere we went. It was perfect, until one night I asked her what she wanted to do after work, and without even flinching she said, "Whatever I feel like doing. We're not dating, you know."

I did not know. It sure felt like dating. But the kicker came next. "My friend Andre is in town from L.A.," she continued, "so I'll talk to you in a couple days."

This was apocalyptic devastation – like finding out there is no Santa Claus, or worse; like finding out there definitely is a Santa Claus and he thinks that you are a total dick.

I walked back inside and saw all the usual Friday night stuff; standing room only frat boys, the fuck faces of the cackling scum who ringed the stage, and a mercenary coven of insincere naked women. But mostly I saw a Greek chorus of me, standing out in the crowd like an oversized Waldo, cringing with disbelief over how totally I'd been played. I just couldn't believe it. How could she be so cavalier? I mean, we were already talking about her quitting dancing and getting a regular job – or at least I was.

I finished my shift, got on my motorcycle, and went for a long ride, which turned into a short ride, which became just my usual three mile commute home. I desperately wanted to be cinematic about it all, but the hurt wouldn't let me imagine myself as anything other than what I was – a fool who ditched a golden opportunity at the Improv to go back to the titty bars and get worked by another stripper. It was excruciating, and worst of all, I had to go home and sleep in the same bed where Edie and I had made sweet, meaningful love all that week and a half ago.

The next morning, I woke up in a rage and decided to go over to her place and demand my television back. She gave it to me, and I stormed down the stairs, remembered that I was on a motorcycle, and threw the fucking thing in the trash. I spent the whole afternoon stomping up and down the mountain, then Dylan and I went and tied one on; which only won me a hangover, and an even larger measure of despair. Then on Sunday, I went back to the office, and that's when I saw her again.

She said she was sorry, and begged me to come over to her place to talk. I told her to fuck off, and wound up going over there on Tuesday instead. Still, I wasn't about to go inside with her; and since my television was in her dumpster, that's where I made my stand.

She pleaded for my forgiveness, literally, and even conjured a few tears - or at least spoke in that whiney voice that kids use when they want their moms to believe that they're crying. But I just laughed. I mean, who in the hell did she think she was talking to? The whole thing was just ridiculous; more than ridiculous – insulting. But the begging was nice, so I allowed her a few more futile beseechings as I prepared to mount my bike and ride off into the night. I figured that watching my taillights disappear down the alley would be a fitting end to the hell she had put me through, and I was relishing that poignant, ironic, poetically just, and fortune reversing image when, all of the sudden, I realized that she was blowing me.

I had no idea how this could have happened, but I did know that one of the girls from the club was in her living room, so this fellatio among the collected refuse of her apartment complex was where the whole sordid business would end. Which was just as good as, if not better than, "Fuck you, I'm out of here," because now I could have my way with her, then gun that throttle, burn some rubber, and ride off satisfied, with my pride fully restored.

Cruel? Maybe; but I never would have considered leaving her in a cloud of dust and gravel if she hadn't done me so wrong; and besides, the new me just was not going to play that shit anymore. It was big boy time, and no longer would I, a former Mr. Teenage Arizona for God's sake, be treated poorly by someone whose primary accomplishment in life was being born attractive.

However, the actual next thing which happened was that we were locked inside her pantry having sex against the shelves while her friend sat on the couch watching MTV.

The point is, everyone deserves a second chance, so we got right back into it again for about three more weeks. There was all kinds of making out in the car, and even more crazy relations at all hours of the day and night, and then there were actual conversations about both of us quitting the club and starting a new life together. She even read me the budget she made for her prospective new reality as a civilian. It included a thousand dollars a month for clothes, five hundred for tanning, hair, and make-up, another thousand for car payment and insurance, twelve hundred for rent, a generous allotment for clubs and travel, and on and on in a similar fashion. Then the all too familiar back and forth:

"What would we do if we left the club?"

"Who cares, we'd have each other."

"Yeah, but like, money; how would we get that?"

"The way everyone else does. We'd get regular jobs, and live our lives."

"Doing what?"

"Why does it matter? I could be happy just living in a trailer with you in Yuma."

"I couldn't."

"So stripping? That's the long term plan?"

"No, I'm going to buy some C.D.'s or something."

"Do you even know what a C.D. is?"

"Fuck you – I'll start a boutique"

"And sell what?"

"I don't know. What the hell is so wrong with dancing anyway?"

"Are you serious?"

"Yeah, it's good exposure."

"Good exposure! In the name of what?"

"It's a profession; like lawyer, or doctor, or artist. I work in a topless dance studio, and I have a regular clientele, and…"

"Okay, I am sorry, but you strip in a titty bar, and your "clientele" are a bunch of horny, drunken dirtheads."

"Fuck you!"

"Fine, fuck me, but I'm right. And there is no future in that place."

And so on, and so forth, until she drops me off in disgust, and later that night I go over to her apartment to talk it out in a more civil tone, and find two guys in her living room. It looks sort of like a drug deal, but it could be anything; and I've had it, so I bolt, and ride around for half an hour screaming in my helmet.

The next three days are filled with loathing. We do not speak, and I make a point of staring at Ashley - the super hot, but way less pretentious, new girl from Washington - every time she is on stage. Edie hates this, probably more because Ashley is getting so much attention in *her* club than because I may have taken an interest in somebody else. And it works, because eventually she approaches with a kind word, and a new version of the same basic thing begins anew.

Only this time it's different; really, because her dad is coming to town, and she is giddy, and absolutely insisting that I meet him. Her enthusiasm is so extreme that I'm beginning to wonder if this has been her ulterior motive all along. I may be a steroidal nightclub bouncer with earrings and drinking issues, but being in college, having an apparently healthy body and a generally friendly disposition makes me look positively All-American next to the other guys in her orbit – particularly that douche, Todd, whom I have never been able to stand. And it could also be that she really likes me, and the settling in process is just bumpy. Who knows. My compass is so completely broken, I doubt if I could find real love if it was standing right next to me under a giant flashing heart. It would, however, be tragic if I dropped her without knowing for sure. So I have to try again.

In advance of her father's visit, Edie is nicer, and she sleeps right next to me at night. We bathe together, and eat dinner out before our shifts, and as she lets her guard down, I start to notice things. Like one day, we are at the Pizza Hut next to the tire place on Scottsdale Road. There is a sign in front of the service bays that reads, "Wheels & Alignment," and she is staring at it, making a weird blowing noise. A little at a time, her breathy sound becomes the word "wheels." Then she goes to work on "alignment," but never quite gets there. Eventually, she looks to me for the answer, and I tell her. She nods, then returns her gaze to the road outside. Her power and confidence are gone, and there is a look on her face that I've never seen before on a grown woman. I want to help, but she has a big ego, so I file it away for some other time, hoping an opportunity will arise when she might want my assistance.

And then, a few days later, we are taking a shower and she tells me that she has had an abortion; not by me, and not even recently – just that this is something from her past which has happened. I nod so that she will know that I understand, and that I certainly am not judging her; and once she sees that I can be trusted with delicate information, she tells me the rest of the story: She has had a bunch of abortions – six, to be exact. I try to keep my poker face, but this confession definitely colors her mood for the rest of the night - and mine too.

I'm really not sure what to make of this new Edie. Maybe she's turning over a new leaf, or maybe she wants to put down her guns and start over; though it is also possible that I am assigning an emotional life to her that isn't really there. It's hard to tell, but as the day of her father's arrival draws near, her excitement becomes almost maniacal. This is a business trip of some stripe, but he is going to stay at her apartment, which seems weird to me. Like, how could a father live – even temporarily – in a place which is paid for by his daughter essentially selling her body? And for that matter, how can I? Of course, this is the wrong time for such a conversation, and I don't want to rain on her parade, so I soldier on, ready to play my part in whatever this introduction brings.

On the night before her dad's arrival, Edie and I are in her bed about to fall asleep. She is happy, so I am happy, and everything is wonderful until a loud clattering from outside kills the moment. It sounds like someone is trying to break in. I look through the blinds, onto the courtyard, and see a man climbing up the side of the building onto her balcony. This is some seriously scary shit; but home court advantage, someone to protect, and overconfidence in the power of my body to intimidate, has me ready for combat. I pull on my pants, she throws me my shirt, but I decide to let the pecs do the talking – hoping he won't answer with a gun or knife.

The man pulls himself over the railing and stands on the other side of the sliding glass door. The curtain is drawn, so he can't see us, but the moonlight behind him shows me exactly where he is. Then he speaks:

"Edie…" he calls, in a loud whisper.

I look to her for an explanation, but she has no idea what's up; or at least that's the story she's going with.

"Edie, baby, let me in."

I glance at her again, this time with all the, "Are you sure there's nothing you want to confess?" I can muster. She shakes her head with apparent sincerity, so I opt to go aggro on this fucker.

With my maximum power scowl, I throw open the curtain and bark, "What in the fuck do you want, asshole!" The prowler jumps backward into the patio furniture, and for the first time, I see his face. It's Todd, that pathetic asshole, and right away he starts begging, "Craig, I'm so sorry, bro. I didn't know, I didn't know."

Thinking he's referring to the fact that he obviously did not know that I was here, I say, "Get the fuck out of here, Todd. We're going to sleep."

Then he continues, "Bro, I swear if I had known that Ttina was your girlfriend, I never would have done it."

And now it all makes sense. He was screwing Ttina when he was the DJ at the Hi-Liter and she was dancing over there. That's where she was at all hours, and because I am a total idiot, I didn't add it up at the time. Actually, I sort of did add it up, and threatened him at a bar one night; but that was one of those "Don't even think about, pal," things - just in case. I guess I was right; which is surprising, but not shocking; and I'm sleeping with his girlfriend now, so fair is fair. I tell him again to get lost, and decide to have sex with Edie again for good measure.

The following afternoon, Edie's dad finally arrives, and as soon as I get off work, she hauls me over to her place to shake his hand. I really am flattered that she wants to include me in this visit, but knowing what I know about strippers' parents (particularly their fathers), I'm not expecting much.

My jaw drops when I finally meet the subject of all this build up, because it's so much worse than I'd guessed. First of all, he is elderly. Easily in his late sixties or early seventies; ugly, fat, and pale. Edie can be so sparkly and sexy, and she's such a natural entertainer, I guess I was expecting someone like George Hamilton or Bob Barker. But this guy; if you walked into a flophouse – like a genuine hotel for indigent men – and just grabbed the first slouch you saw, he would be a thousand times more charismatic and emotionally available than this dead eyed geezer. And still she is bouncing around, thrilled just to be in his presence. She introduces me, and I smile and try to engage him in a little small talk, and get absolutely nothing in return. Just a cold fish, weak old man handshake, and a little bit of a sneer. He doesn't speak; not even to her, and all I want is to run for the door. And so I do, at the first available opportunity, which doesn't seem to bother Edie at all. She is going to cook a big dinner for her daddy (as she repeatedly calls him), and I had no idea that she even knew how to cook.

**

I don't see or hear from Edie for several days, and when I do, she is much more subdued than the person I've been hanging out with lately. Her dad is gone, and who knows what happened while he was here. I can't even bring myself to ask. At work that night, she is a million miles from the star who normally lights up the big stage at Candy's. Just deflated. Which is alarming, because if anyone ever looked at this job as a show, it was her; and if anyone ever enjoyed being the queen of a shitty little club in a mid-sized city more, then I never met them.

She came back after a while, and there were nights when she would even be the super star again, but her days as the undisputed heavyweight champion of Scottsdale Road were basically ending right in front of me.

We went out later that week, about as far from Scottsdale as we had ever been – though that was really just north Tempe, up around Baseline. She didn't want to drive her car, so we rode my bike up there - neither of us in a helmet - and saw a movie. She was still relatively sedate, and when the film started she got in my lap and curled up like a little kid. And then I was bummed, because we were basically alone in the theater, miles from that fucking bar, and this was the moment I would have killed for just a few weeks prior; but it was obvious that we'd never be able to sustain it.

8

SLOPPY

As Edie drifted off into a rave and drug world ether that was only one of her many secrets, my emotional state collapsed. That two-month roller coaster ride was taxing, but the moments of exhilaration, and hope, and even catastrophe gave me a reprieve from the free fall I was experiencing before it started. Edie was chaos, but focusing on someone else's problems instead of my own had helped in ways that I didn't realize even as I began to drink heavily and use coke on the clock.

It was almost impossible to get fired at Candy's because no one was really steering the ship. Wayne, the guy who owned the place, was a big partier, and when he could convince one of the girls to sleep with him, you wouldn't see him, or the lucky gal, for weeks on end. He did, however, hire Wallace - the only man in all of Phoenix who walked around in a boat captain's hat – as a "manager," but Wallace was an old, drunken homunculus who lived on the fumes of sex with dancers which never actually materialized; and as far as I could tell, his duties were either drinking alone in the back office, or drinking alone at the bar. It must have been exhausting too, because he would frequently duck out to go to God knows where, and then not return at the end of the night.

It was a lawless situation. Girls were getting high in the toilet, and guys stealing cover charges, passing out free drinks, and even breaking into the cars in the lot. And sometimes I'd be so sloppy that I'd slur at the customers, and make a point of calling them "dirthead" in an inebriated attempt to make Troy laugh.

One Thursday, I got way too drunk, so the guys let me sneak out the back door and go home early. It was about eleven o'clock, and for a moment, it seemed like my bad decision making had brought me some good luck, when Edie volunteered to drive me home. But as we walked outside, a bunch of guys started hollering at her. It was the usual shit, but I got into a shouting match with them, and they followed us when we left. A couple miles down the road, near the Devil House, we hit a traffic light, and I jumped out and got into a fight with a guy who was a good five inches taller than me. My reflexes were slow, and I was about to get my ass kicked, when a good Samaritan ran out of a store, screaming that he had called the cops. "Praise Jesus," was about the only thing going through my mind as I dove back into Edie's car with at least some of my dignity intact; and when she ditched me at my doorstep without so much as a kiss good-night, it began to occur to me that perhaps I was getting a little reckless.

My life, as they say in A.A., was getting unmanageable. My grades were slipping, and I was spending most of the day having the imaginary dialogue with my father, where he criticizes, I agree, and then bargain and promise to achieve more as a redemptive act of penance. There was a bodybuilding show coming up in San Diego, and though my dad absolutely hated bodybuilding, and had chastised me for even attending shows, I started thinking maybe I would enter as a way to get myself back on track. Still, my habits at the club, and the pot smoking I was doing at home – even though I had long since ceased to enjoy the feeling of smoking weed – was running me down. And then, just as that hopelessness was starting to fit me like an ugly old coat, an inspiring new face appeared at the club. But this person wasn't a dancer, or even a female; he was a five year-old boy named Aaron.

I met Amy, Aaron's mom, during my first week at Bourbon Street. Amy was tough, and smart, and for years whenever I saw her I flashed on our first conversation, when she showed me a couple of welts on her ass, then bragged that they were the result of kinky, hanger wielding sex she'd had with an entire rock band. She was obviously trying to shock, and also, obviously telling the truth; but I liked her, and felt an inexplicable kinship with her, even though we were really more acquaintances than friends.

A couple of years down the line, when Amy hired on at Candy's, I began to fill in the blanks of this kinship when I realized that Amy's mom, Geena, was the same Geena who had been dating my best friend, Dylan, for the past year and a half. Geena had always reminded me so much of my own mom, that when Amy told me she was Geena's daughter, I wanted to pick her up and hug her. We dove right into a commiseration over how grossed out we were by this relationship, and in so doing, realized that we had other stuff in common too. Just starting with the obvious – that both of our moms were attractive blondes in their early forties dating oversized young guys - we had clearly had similar backgrounds, peppered with an abundance of horny mother chasers. And there was other overlap. We were both huge rock'n'roll fans, we were the same age, we worked at the same places, and her half-sister, Tammy – a dancer and Hustler model - was one of the girls I'd met at the Iron Maiden concert, years prior, who got me started in this business in the first place.

This older Amy was cooler too. Cigarettes had made her voice huskier, and settling into motherhood had given her a gravity that none of the other girls had. Which is not to imply that she was settled – because that was far from the case – only that she had this boundary around her child that made her seem more grown up. Amy also didn't need to shock anymore. She was strong and she knew who she was, and I felt proud that while everyone else used her stage name, I called her by her given one, which was like our secret handshake. But I never seriously considered going out with Amy because, I guess, my feelings toward her were more brotherly. She was also into rocker guys in a big way, and she was a mom – and I absolutely did not want to be one of those guys who came around and made nice in order to get in your mother's pants.

Still, Amy and I did wander briefly into that arena when Geena started working at the club. She and her mother would alternate shifts (though they also worked together, which I never got used to) three or four nights a week; and they would pass Aaron off to each other as one clocked in and the other clocked out. This was my shift change as well, so I would often be outside when they were doing the switch. And always, the same thought would occur to me - "Good God, that's me and my mom times two!"

The parent/child chemistry between Amy and Geena was uncomfortably familiar to me, and they were both dead ringers for my mother at different ages. But when I met Aaron, and saw him with Amy, about a dozen family photo albums shot through my head. I couldn't look at the two of them together and not see pictures of me and my mom at the same age, and his blonde hair and green eyes even made him look like me back then.

He was such a friendly little guy, and I started really looking forward to seeing him. His grandma and mom and I would hang out by the donut shop and talk, or I'd give him rides around the lot on my motorcycle. And if I wasn't outside when they arrived, Geena or Amy would usually come and get me so that he could sing "Friends In Low Places" to me, or just say hello.

And as the sleaziness of that life was running me down, seeing Aaron would remind me of what I'd been after all along – a family of my own.

Eventually, Geena began pushing me to ask Amy out, and I could tell Amy was up for it too; although I was fairly certain her interest had more to do with wanting a father for her son than some outsized attraction for me. Her type was rockers, and she was always flying off to L.A. to hang out with this band or that singer, and there was even a rumor that Aaron was the illegitimate son of Sebastian

Bach from Skid Row. But even though I knew this wasn't going to end in anything long-term, I gradually became enamored of the idea of picking up Amy and Aaron and taking them to the movies. It seemed so grown up and positive, and since I wasn't making many good decisions at the time, I figured it certainly couldn't hurt.

Amy and I decided that we'd take Aaron to see *Home Alone*, and for the next week or so, I got a strong feeling of paternal responsibility whenever I saw them. I was no actual part of their family, but I loved being, in some peripheral way, a good person in their lives.

Edie, on the other hand, didn't care for my friendship with Amy at all. We weren't seeing each other anymore, but my attraction to her hadn't waned; and I still secretly hoped that somehow, some way, I could save her from herself, and magically fix all the problems in her life. At the very least, and for reasons already addressed, I would happily have gone to work full bore on her life, if only to take my mind off of my own.

As the week wore on, Edie moved in. She was flirtatious and sweet, but I never saw her attention and my plans with Amy as related. One was a healthy, happy, responsible step out of the norm for me, my friend, and her son, and the other was a garden variety, self-destructive, and often humiliating, sexual obsession. Taking a little boy to the movies seemed like something the whole world would root for, while revisiting the darkest and most complicated corners of my libido in the waning days of a tormented affair, seemed like something you do in spite of yourself (which, of course, it almost always is).

When Monday finally arrived, I got an early morning call from Edie. She was inviting me over to hang out, and since I didn't have to pick up Amy and Aaron until seven, I figured why not. But almost as soon as I walked in her door, the shenanigans commenced. And by shenanigans, I mean Olympic level sexual intercourse.

The fornication went on for hours, and when the first round ended, and I walked into her kitchen to get a drink of water from her faucet, she hit me with the real reason for her invitation.

"Don't go with her tonight," she said, and stared into my eyes with nasty promise.

"What's the big deal? We're just seeing *Home Alone* with her little boy."

She came in closer. "Don't go," she whispered, and pulled me down on top of her next to the refrigerator. And then it was on again – in the kitchen, in the living room, and back in the bedroom – and when that was over, she said, "Stay with me tonight, and we'll go to Prescott or Flagstaff and I'll rent us a room for few days."

An impromptu vacation with Edie sounded wonderful, but ditching a little boy and his mom seemed like the kind of thing only a full blown asshole would do. So I said, "Edie, it's just for a few hours. We're going to have popcorn and watch a movie, then I'll come right back.

"No... Please." She looked so hurt, but I couldn't figure out why. We hadn't been seeing each other for like a month, and until she found out about Amy, she hadn't shown much interest in me at all.

"Edie, I can't ditch a little boy and his mom. If you want to talk about getting back together, then we can do that tonight, okay."

But it wasn't okay. She stopped talking, and though it was raining, I could tell it was time to get on my bike and ride. It was baffling to me that she could be threatened by something so innocent, but I guess I wasn't thinking like a woman; I was thinking like a young guy, for whom sex is often the defining factor of a relationship.

Hanging out with Aaron and Amy, on the other hand, was wonderful. I had no ulterior motive, so I was able to totally enjoy being with them. And walking around with a boy and his mom for the first time made me feel ten feet tall. Just buying popcorn and sodas for us at the concession stand was a revelation. It was such a small thing, dollars and effort-wise, but it made me feel so grown up and – decent, for lack of a better word.

As we walked through the lobby and took our seats, I paid attention to the way we were being perceived. People get defensive around a young guy, and they instinctively keep their distance. With a bunch of guys, that feeling rises exponentially with the addition of each male member of the group. A young couple calms people down a little, but the energy around a young family is clean and inviting, and again, so adult in a bright, warm, and positive way.

It was more like being in a movie than watching one, and I enjoyed every detail. I saw Aaron eating the popcorn I bought him, and felt so proud. I glanced at Amy's face, and she looked relieved and happy. Then I realized that for the first time in a long time, I was truly unconflicted about myself.

It was like before Andie got pregnant, when I could still fantasize about quitting all my bad habits, and, at sixteen, becoming a great husband and father overnight; except this seemed actually possible. And I thought, if there was some way to become this man in the long-term - and this evening was probably the first time I ever really felt like a man — then that's what I wanted to do.

The whole night lasted maybe four hours, then I drove home, returned my roommate's car, and went to bed visualizing the person I wanted to become. However, I also knew that continuing much further down the after-work path with Amy would be misleading to her and her son; so, in spite of the amazing inspiration this relatively quick date provided, we didn't go on that way together.

9

THE LAST MUSCLE SHOW

I am back in the gym full time now, and working harder than ever. I've decided to enter the show in San Diego, and though I know I can't win – my roommate, Jerry, who looks like Frank Zane, is also entering – I want to do as well as possible because I think this may be it for me. Bodybuilding has been my savior and my identity, and it has taught me discipline and focus (if only in fits and bursts), but the drugs, and diet, and tanning, and hours upon hours in the weight pile don't necessarily match up with the image of myself I saw in the movie theater with Amy and Aaron. I don't really understand it, but here lately, I've been feeling like a lizard must when it wants to shed its skin.

Lizards have it easy, though, because they pretty much know what's underneath the old lizard skin (new lizard skin). I, on the other hand, do not have a clear sense of what's next. Maybe this feeling will pass. Maybe I'll go back to being the same guy I have always been, just older. Who knows. The only thing I'm really sure about is that the farther I walk in the direction of this new feeling, the more I like it, and the more I want to shake off the person I used to be.

On the upside, fear of standing before large crowds of people in my underwear and looking ridiculous has driven me off of alcohol and narcotics. Contest dieting, and the tunnel vision that comes with it, has pushed my sex drive into the storage bin of my mind, and that is keeping me out of trouble with the dancers at the club. Ashley is probably the only girl I'd break down for at this point, and she lives with her boyfriend - which isn't that big a deal in our world, but it helps me to believe that I am off the hook, at least for now.

My clear head is making it harder to go to work, though. The more I'm there, the more I see it as a sad and vicious wheel of manipulation. I know too much about the girls and myself now to pretend that we are a tribe of anything anymore. Molestation and parental neglect is what we share – period – and that's nothing to build a life on. That kind of shit is fuel, and you can either douse yourself in it and light a match; or you can pour it in the tank and let it power your drive to a better place.

I stand in this bar night after night, and day after day, sometimes fourteen hours at a stretch, and I see traumatized little girls acting out control fantasies over men, and confused little boys on a demented quest for intimacy. Maybe this doesn't apply to everyone, but to the chronic participants in this obsessive little universe, it certainly does. And nudity is the glue that holds it all together. Nudity that these girls offer in exchange for money, adulation, and false feelings of acceptance, power, and security. And nudity which implies intimacy and trust and sex in the male brain; which, of course, is the very trick that keeps these clubs in business.

I hear people say that these places are bastions of feminist empowerment, and that the girls are really holding all the cards because they are playing the men for fools. Or there is the myth of the college student stripper, or the dancer who packs away the bucks and owns a vacation home in the Tropics. All bullshit. I never met a stripper who was truly working toward an actual four-year degree in any meaningful way. I have, however, encountered a few who were pushing thirty and decided to go to a seven month trade school to become a veterinary tech, or a dental hygienist, or stenographer or something, but inevitably their graduation plan - to dance a couple of nights as they phase into their new life - ends when they realize that a single table dance equals two hours pay at the new place. And the same goes for the club owners, and the bouncers, and the hardcore regulars. Everyone loses in the end, because this kind of sleaziness is a tar pit, and no amount of rationalizing turns a cesspool into the Blue Lagoon.

Big Earl told me on my first day of work, "You're gonna get so much pussy in here," and he wasn't kidding. I have definitely gotten a whole lot of pussy - in exactly the same way that the dying miners in *The Treasure of the Sierra Madre* found a whole lot of gold, or the old man in Hemingway's book landed a really big fish. But what has it earned me, and am I really going to stay here and die for something that I can't take any comfort in, and doesn't even mean what I wish it did?

I think about this on the drive out to California. It's weird, because even though this journey is a bit of a convoy - with Ray driving me, Dylan riding with his girlfriend, some guys from the gym trailing us, and Jerry and his new woman in the back - it feels much lonelier than the trip Ttina and I took just a year and a half ago.

The sensation of crossing out of a valley nags at me. And there is a heavy sadness like I used to feel right before we'd move in the old days. Nothing is wrong, though. To the contrary, everything is going about as good as can be expected. I bunk with Ray, and do well in the show — second in my class — and afterwards I spend an evening running around the Tijuana strip club/whorehouses with my buddies.

My reasons for doing this have everything to do with habit, and nothing really to do with sex. And the state of these places just underscores the feeling I've been having for the past couple of months.

The strip clubs in Tijuana double as brothels, and they are the kind of sleazy which makes seedy places think that maybe they're not so seedy after all. The rooms are like zombie saloons, and a scratchy, vinyl Air Supply album plays from first track to last through a blown speaker on the bar. The dancers — really just exhausted prostitutes - writhe around on stage, obviously wishing they were anywhere but here, and suddenly it occurs to you — or, at least, it occurs to me — that your life has become the scene in *The Shining* where Jack Nicholson encounters the beautiful woman in the bathtub. She rises, glistening and beautiful, and he takes her in his arms. Then, as they are making out, he glances in the mirror and sees that she has transformed into a hideous, cackling hag.

It's just awful; so bad, as a matter of fact, that you decide, along with one of your friends, to go and get your other friend out of the room where he is currently making sweet love from behind with a sad eyed lady of the evening. And though this costs you five dollars paid to another prostitute to open the hallway door, it would be worth it at twice the price, because these are the moments which remind you that the sex business is either tragically hilarious, or hilariously tragic, and that either way, the time is nigh for a thinking person to seriously consider heading for the exit.

10

DONUTS

Ruth, the sweet, old, bald woman who runs the Dunkin Donuts at night, looks at me funny when I come in here now; and that is because Ruth is no dummy. I show up at least three times an evening to use their bathroom, and there is a perfectly good toilet next door (several, as a matter of fact). So Ruth has deduced, accurately, that my appearances must mean one of two things – ongoing intestinal distress or drugs.

It's drugs.

I never thought I'd get myself into a situation where the best part of my night would be sitting in the ghost of someone else's bowel movement and snorting coke off the top of a donut shop commode. But that's what it's come to. I'm still full of ideas about the future, but the temptations of the present combined with hours upon hours of nothing to do but watch strippers and drunks has thrown a serious wrench into my self improvement project.

I am, in my quiet moments, a little alarmed, because the portion of my life spent under the influence of alcohol and cocaine is growing rapidly, and I'm not completely sure how that happened, especially when I could finally see the light at the end of the tunnel.

I wasn't going to do all these things together, but pot and steroids have no hazardous interactivity issues, so I guess I gradually figured why not. Coke was a bigger decision – but not a hell of a lot bigger. Lots of guys at the gym, particularly the ones who compete in shows, and some of the professional wrestlers who pass through town, use crank and steroids simultaneously to grow, suppress their appetite, and speed up their metabolism. I'm no doctor, but enlarging your heart and speeding it up at the same time has always sounded like a recipe for disaster to me, but with coke I was eventually able to tell myself that it was more a byproduct of a boring night, than a mad scientist's mixture of muscle building chemicals.

Drinking and taking steroids is another combination I thought I'd never indulge because they are both so bad for your liver. I don't have a great excuse for this one, except that you can't see your liver (or your heart), so, out of sight, out of mind, I guess. But sometimes when I'm drinking, particularly here at Candy's, part of me is standing off to the side wondering why I'm being so reckless just because I can.

I've been bartending lately too. It's a way for the club to cut expenses by having me work slower shifts as both security and booze dispenser. I don't mind; I make more money this way. It's boring, though; and sometimes the girls and I will get drunk just because there is booze available to drink. The adult supervision in this place is laughable, but when the position of adult falls on me, as it occasionally does now, it can get borderline hysterical. Not that either of our managers care. When Jason works I get tipped out from his cover charge stealing and credit card fraud side projects, and when Wallace is here, he is my best customer. No one gives a shit, so why not mess around with girls in the beer closet, or do lines with Ritchie, or pollute my body when I'm supposed to be working? And, of course, the reason why not is because time's a wastin'.

I'm twenty-one and a half now — and probably closer to three quarters. I'm not a child, which makes it harder and harder to rationalize this behavior.

I went to go see Emily's new kitten, Fluffy, the other day, and I felt like a roaring hypocrite. I've seen myself as a kind of role model and quasi-parent to her, and I'm so full of bad habits at the moment, the best I can offer is an ingratiating impersonation of the kind of adult she needs in her life. I can smile and tell her how cute the kitten is, but in my heart I know that the moral authority grown-ups need to guide the children who look up to them is slipping away from me fast.

When I think about all the crap I'm pumping into my body in the name of having a good time or looking like a superhero, and the thirty or so hours a week I spend in a throbbing quagmire of the human condition, it seems almost criminally stupid, because now I know better, and I have seen the light. There is a better and more admirable way, one that matches up with the ideals and dreams I've had since Edmond, it's just that dropping bad habits and defense mechanisms is a lot harder than it ought to be.

I want to walk away, but it's so easy now. I have no fear of the opposite sex, drugs of every stripe are available for the asking, and my steroid enhanced body, which draws a lot of this stuff to me, is a big chunk of my identity. I've been in the nightclub business a long time, relatively speaking; and if you add this to years spent in the bodybuilding gyms, I'm in a position now where I know people at most every bar in town, and almost never have to deal with a line or a cover charge, or even paying for drinks. I simply do not have to address my shortcomings at the moment if I don't want to.

But these facts remain; I know I am supposed to be a father some day, and I am definitely not moving in the direction that young men must move in order to be good parents. I am no longer among the youngest people in this club or this business – which may be a subtle shading at the moment, but I know too many tired, old twenty-eight year-old dancers to believe that this difference will remain subtle for long. I'm also ignoring the passion I used to feel for music, movies, books and life in general. And to this end, I am surrounded by people who not only do not inspire me, but constantly remind me how far off track I've gotten.

I don't even see the sexy part of this place anymore, just the frustration and desperation. The boobs are like wallpaper now, and it's the faces of the construction workers who have spent their week's pay on a few hours of drunken titillation that stand out. Or maybe it's the red-faced lush that owns the bar next door who comes over in the afternoon and pays the DJ to play *Something to Believe In* five times in a row, or the gimpy kid who stays until we toss him out for being too drunk – though he always arrives in that condition and never spends a penny. Somebody beat him up and robbed him in Old Towne a couple nights ago, and he limped here from a mile away to ask for help. I felt bad for him, so I drove him to the hospital, and along the way I realized that this guy has no one. Some parent, or parents, just tossed this pathetic creature out into the world and expected him to find his way.

And there are worse stories too. I took one of our problem drinkers home the other day. He'd been in here swilling five-dollar beers for most of the afternoon, and was falling asleep at his table - not unusual for this older, and almost totally nonverbal man. It was getting dark, and I was off for the night, so I drove him to his trailer park, and helped him to his door. Inside, I found one of the skeezy day girls living there with her even more skuzzy boyfriend, and her four year-old kid. They had clearly moved in on this hapless, retired auto mechanic, and were milking him for all he was worth.

Someday, I will leave, though. I'm sure of it. And I pray that once I'm gone, the sound of Poison, Warrant, Def Leppard, and Winger will leave my head forever. But there is one song that I'm sure has scarred my mind permanently, and will never leave, no matter how hard I try to banish it. *Bad To The Bone*, written by Satan through George Thorogood, is the centerpiece of every bachelor party that stumbles in the door. Four or five times a night, some drunken, groom-to-be is pushed on stage, seated in a bar chair, and heckled by Ritchie, while four girls dance around him to the sound of *Bad To The Godforsaken Bone*. This happens so much it reminds me of the way they tortured Noriega by blasting rock music into his palace until he gave himself up. But the thing that bothers me most about the whole fucking thing, aside from the grinding repetition of it all, is that they always choose Ashley to go up there, and she is way too smart and beautiful for this dump.

11

ASHLEY

She is blonde, and one of the only girls I know in this business who doesn't have a gigantic Aquanet sculpture of hair and an obvious boob job (or any boob job at all, for that matter). She is smart. She doesn't hang out with the other girls, and she doesn't seem to be into partying. She worked at a heavier place in Seattle, but if I met her somewhere else, I would never have marked her for this type of work. And, of course, by the time I've given it this much thought, I already know that I am fucked, and headed back down the dancer path again.

We're going to lunch this afternoon; and if you consider that it's Valentine's Day, then this courtship – if you can call a first date a courtship – has already taken an unprecedented turn. A daylight get together is usually way down the road for me, and starting here is sort of novel. But if you told me that I'd have this girl pregnant and married in seven months, I'd say you were probably even crazier than I am, yet that's exactly where this otherwise inconsequential meal leads – and then on and on, in one way or the other, for the remainder of my days.

12

WHAT YOU WISH FOR

It all happened so fast. One minute I was performing the greatest hits of my "Now that we're sleeping together, wayward dancer, why don't you change your life in the following ways," routine, and the next minute the tables had turned. It began at Denny's a couple of weeks after our first date. We were having a post shift breakfast, and I decided to give her a little surprise. I had a half an eight ball in my pocket, so while we were waiting for our Moons Over My Hammy, I said, "Hey, Ashley, do you want to do some coke?" And do you know what she said? "No."

And this wasn't a garden variety, I prefer not to, kind of "No." It was "No," combined with the sort of disgusted and baffled look you'd get if you invited a woman to go grave robbing with you. Which was stunning, because nobody else in that bar would have turned down free, out of the blue, cocaine, and here it was happening right in front of me.

It was so bizarre, as a matter of fact, that it almost seemed like she was speaking a foreign language. But then it occurred to me, "No, no, no... Sanity - that's what this is." And once I had a second to digest her response, I decided to take a leap of faith.

"Let's go throw this away. I don't need it."

She looked at me for a second, trying to decide if I was on the level, and then she said, "Okay." And just like that, we were walking outside to the dumpster and disposing of a hundred twenty-five dollars worth of narcotics.

It was a good feeling, but frightening too, because this relationship had the heavy vibe of fate from the very beginning. Being with Ashley was like the positive – but no less intimidating - version of walking past a dark alley in an unfamiliar city and sensing the strong presence of danger; and for the first time since my first time, I was terrified to sleep with someone.

If we had gone on two more dates without me making a move, she probably would've written me off as gay. Then, when we finally did work our way around to the inevitable, the word "home" kept floating through my brain. I can't explain it, so I won't even try, but it had nothing to do with anything freaky, or forced, or drug related, or even any desire to end a long journey. It just felt strange – kind of like an arrival in the same way that my trip to Florida five years earlier had an overpowering sense of launch. And oddly, all of the stuff I'd accumulated as a result of that trip – topless bars, crazy girls, cocaine, steroids, my inflated body and self image - started to fall away like the stages of a rocket.

After the coke thing, we double dated with Dylan, and went to a Rory Gallagher show at Gibsons. We were smashed; so drunk, in fact, that she got sick in the middle of the night. And suddenly, we weren't drinking anymore.

Three or four days after that, I pulled my shoebox of steroids out from under the bed, and took a long look at the syringes and vials and pills inside. Now seemed like as good a time as any to continue an apparently productive trend, so I walked outside and tossed another hundred fifty dollars worth of contraband into yet another dumpster.

Every day it seemed like we'd shed another layer of skin, and sometimes very abruptly. One day, around this time, she was dancing for a group of guys near the main stage when one of them touched her. It wasn't a big deal, but it was definitely against the rules. She brushed him off, and I, pouring drinks over the wash sink, tried to keep my cool. But then he did it again, and before I knew what was happening, I was flying over the bar and bashing the guy's head against the stage. Troy pulled me off of him, and I didn't get fired, or even talked to by anyone, but it was clear that this situation was not working.

After that, I told Ashley, predictably, that I desperately wanted her to stop dancing, and to my surprise, she stopped. Then, after a brief period of her cocktail waitressing at the club, the hellacious withdrawal stage of our brand new relationship officially got underway.

Old habits die hard, and when your identity, and your job, and your friends, and your defense mechanisms, and your lifestyle, and your addictions are all wrapped up in those habits, and the whole mess is tied together with spasms of who knows what bubbling up from your dark and ancient history, things can get testy and depressing in a hurry, and man did they ever.

For years I got bigger and stronger every time I walked into a gym, and suddenly, I was shrinking - fast. About every two weeks I'd lose another five pounds, until I'd dropped from a Herculean two thirty to a totally mortal one ninety-five. And it wasn't for lack of trying. I knew when I quit steroids that some level of atrophy was on its way, so I was hitting the gym with everything I had, hoping to mitigate the downturn. But it didn't work - and my abilities and muscle size seemed to deteriorate every time I passed a mirror.

At the same time, Ashley went to sleep and stayed there for most of the day, which was difficult for me to understand. What was there to miss about stripping – the dirtheads, the manipulation, the exhibitionism – I absolutely did not get it. Of course, the answer was her independence, but I couldn't accept that. She was probably the only dancer I ever knew who had an apartment full of furniture, two cars, and a closet full of attractive clothes which didn't look like something an upscale call girl would wear. But to me, dancing was a horrible sickness you fall into because of desperation and dysfunction, and in a deeply earnest way, I wanted her to appreciate me for bringing the cure. It was basically the same feeling that the character in the song *Roxanne* has. And I almost wanted to say to her, "Look, you don't have to put on the red light because I'm saving you from all that – so would you please quit looking back!"

It wasn't enough that she had stopped. I wanted her to be sorry for it, and I wanted her to acknowledge the amazing piece of rescuing I was doing. As a matter of fact, I wanted her to regret her entire sexual history before me, because, I guess, this was the only way that I could turn her into this angel with a broken wing who would be entirely dependent on me – and therefore never leave.

It wasn't all born of insecurity, though. I really thought I was helping, and I was baffled that when I'd wake up early and go to campus to gather up admittance forms, class schedules, and financial aid information, and have it back on the kitchen table before she woke up, that she wouldn't be happy about this at all.

In the meantime, her influence kept working on me. I cut my hair, took out all of my earrings, and sold the motorcycle. My grades went up, I made it to class more, and I tried to spring toward the light. I was still working at Candy's, but I'd lost so much weight that I wasn't pulling many bouncing shifts; and gradually, as newer and younger guys came to work the door, I became a full time bartender.

The changes kept right on coming, too.

My stock went down in the gym, my self-image started to plummet, and people reacted differently at the club when it was time to lay down the law. If I hadn't realized the free pass I was getting because of my size before, I was getting a crash course in it now.

And then there was Ashley, back at home and never leaving. I'd get up in the morning, go to the gym and school, and come home and she'd still be sleeping. The rest of the day would be cool, but she wasn't working, or hanging out with friends, and I was starting to get worried. Maybe a different couple of people would have called it off at this point, but we had both already changed so much -

not to mention promised each other that we were getting married - that it seemed like there was no turning back. She didn't want to return to the club, and I didn't have any real desire to go back to partying and doing steroids. There was just no point. The bouncing life has a very low ceiling, and there was zero chance that I was going to make it as a professional bodybuilder; plus musclemen were already starting to get sick and drop dead from extreme steroid and stimulant use, so the writing was on the wall.

Once again, my whole life started to feel like baby stuff. Like when you're a kid and all the sudden you don't want to hold you mom's hand in public anymore, or even be seen with her out on the street. A bolt of lightening had hit me, and when I got up and dusted myself off, I realized that I was living someone else's life – and this other guy was younger, dumber, and more reckless than me.

The transition was about as comfortable as being born, and there were moments of panic in every single day where I wanted to run for the hills. It was May, and I could still look back to February and see the big, powerful, white knight I thought I was. And now, I was naked, with no armor, no horse, and no shield - just like everyone else in the world.

Then Ashley got pregnant, and I felt this new, unvarnished, reality-based life begin to solidify around me. I was thrilled at the prospect of becoming a father, and finally having my own family. And I really loved Ashley; but there was so much changing going on - the kind that would be embarrassing even if you were alone on a desert island. And having your limitations and delusions revealed right out in the open can make you resent the people who are watching it happen.

Then the fingers of Fate snapped again, and we went from living in Tempe across from the campus, to unflavored, soul crushing suburbia – directly across the street from my mother and Ray, no less – in Mesa.

Why on earth this seemed like a good idea, I can't even fathom, but it definitely knocked me the rest of the way down from Superman to Clark Kent. And the whole thing – new body, new hair, no earrings, no motorcycle, no partying, no hanging out with friends, no sleeping around, no bouncing, no hours upon hours at the gym, our new residence in a new town, and impending marriage and fatherhood – was done before I finished the classes I was taking when it started.

13

CAMELBACK MOUNTAIN

We drive up on Camelback Mountain to ogle the mansions, look out over the city, and dream about the future. I can't get over how fast life happens. Five minutes ago, I was nine, and riding my bicycle up here to get away from my parents' insanity; and now, here I am with my pregnant wife-to-be, talking about our wedding, which is less than a month and a half away.

I wish we could stay up here all day, seriously, because whatever I was hoping to accomplish by moving down the block from my mother – being closer to Emily, or maybe building a relationship with Mom in advance of the baby coming – is not happening. I see a glimmer of something here and there in her, but it's always lost in a laser light show of dense, foggy, phoniness.

And there's Ray too. Funny how dropping forty pounds of muscle can clarify your standing with the people around you. That guy hates me, and this is yet another reason why I wish we hadn't moved here.

Pretty much the only thing which has worked out is Emily, who brings Fluffy, her cat, over all the time to hang out with Ashley and me. I love Emily so much, and feeling the way I do about her, and about Ashley, is almost enough to make me forget about being the travel-sized and neutered version of the boy I used to be, and start looking ahead to being the man I've been trying to become in fits and bursts all my life. It's a shit idea to look at adulthood as this incredibly deflating shrinking process, and if that wasn't what was literally happening to me at the moment, I think one hundred percent of my energy would be focused on the joy of becoming a dad. Maybe it's like this for everyone, you know; just hard to grow up and start taking life seriously. I'm not sure, but it's not like we have much choice, so may as well get started.

***

When we get home, I walk over to Mom's house to see Emily. There is a strange feeling in the air, and Mom is being very matter of fact about it, which is never a good sign. We talk in the kitchen for a half a minute, and as I walk toward Emily's room, she says, "Don't say anything. Just don't say anything at all."

I have, of course, no idea what she's talking about until I look down and see Fluffy lying in a cardboard box with the back half of her body smashed. The cat has obviously been hit by a car, and she is panting, just barely hanging on, and appears to have been in this condition for a while. It is appalling, and I don't even have time to ask any of the obvious questions, when Mom says, "Ray doesn't want to take it to the vet because it costs too much money, so just don't say anything."

"Mom," say I, in the tone I reserve for occasions when she has clearly parted company with her soul and conscience, "how long has she been like this?"

"Two days."

"Two days!"

"Just leave," says Mom to me as Emily turns the corner. My little sister's face is contorted with sadness and confusion, and it's clear that she has also been told not to comment. So, rather than talk any further to a crazy woman, I pick up the cat in its box and drive it to the closest vet. When I get home, I call Mom to tell her where the cat is. She is furious, and wants the number for the doctor. I give it to her, and that is pretty much that for the next couple of hours.

Ashley and I leave for a while to run errands, and no sooner have we returned than I get a screaming phone call from Ray promising to beat my ass the next time he sees me. We get into a big argument over the phone, and without considering the consequences, I walk over to their house to tell him what a complete asshole he is to let a pet die slowly in front of his daughter.

He pounces as soon as I walk in the door, and immediately I am standing in my mother's kitchen absorbing haymakers to the face thrown by her husband. As usual, she says and does nothing, and this time there is nothing I can do either. My arms are frozen to my sides. I can't even lift them to block the punches because something in the middle of my brain is telling me not to. Maybe it's the quasi-parent thing, maybe it's the shock of it all, or maybe it's simple fear, but the end result is that after all these years of being a tough guy, the only defense I can muster is to stand my ground and refuse to go down.

There is an even bigger problem, though. Mom has bolted from the kitchen and left Emily in the battle zone. Ray isn't about to stop, and this shit is getting out of control in a hurry. A five year-old girl is screaming our names just a few inches from the worst of it, and I fear that if Ray is able to knock me over, or if he changes position, I won't be able to do anything but watch as this nightmare lands on top of her.

And then, a miracle happens. I glance to the side and see Ashley charging into the kitchen, pregnant as hell, scooping Emily up and whisking her out of the house. The relief, even as the blows rain down, is considerable, and it loosens me up enough to move toward the door.

I take about five steps backward, and then I'm out of the house; but Ray follows me onto the driveway and keeps on swinging. Someone yells that they are calling the cops, and I fear that Ray is going to ignore this warning because the punches are still coming, and he's taunting me in a little boy's scream, "Come on, tough guy! Come on, bad ass! Do something, do something!" But I can't; though I'm more sure than ever that there is no way I'm going to let him knock me down, no matter what happens. And then, the cop warning seems to sink in, Ray stops punching me, marches back inside, and slams the door.

There is an eerie calm when he goes. I look around, and it seems like strangers are standing around gawking, but they are just hazy yellow figures that I can't exactly make out. I'm too rattled to tell if they are real or imaginary, and all I want is to get the hell out of here. I stagger back to our condo. Mom and Emily are there with Ashley, and as I approach, Mom runs up and makes a fuss over me. But I don't buy it. I think she may have set me up to do the dirty work on this cat thing, knowing that Ray would blow up, so that she could then swoop in and withhold approval from him until regret finally sunk in, thereby restoring the upper hand in her relationship, and the more compliant Ray. Or perhaps she was thinking that I would humble him. As usual, either way she wins.

And now sirens are screaming down the road. Without missing a beat, Mom walks back to her house and leaves Emily with us. I'm fairly certain that the next thing to happen is that Ray will disappear in a cop car, but when the police come to talk to me they say that Mom didn't see who threw the first punch. And since I didn't throw any punches, it is abundantly clear that my mother has lied to the cops again.

A paramedic looks at the cuts on my face. There is some bruising, and a little blood, but nothing major, so they leave. Then Mom returns, and without saying a word, takes Emily by the hand and starts to walk back across the street. "Mom," I say, "please don't go. You guys can stay here tonight, and we'll figure this out in the morning."

"No, I can't, sweetie." she says, picking her lip.

"Yes, you can! We can stop this craziness right now. You and Emily can move in with me and Ashley for as long as you need to, and then we can start over."

She doesn't answer; at least not with words. She just shakes her head, and walks away with Emily.

And now I finally get it. This is who she has always been, and who she will always be. You can't change her, or save her, because loving her is not about love to her. It's about propping up the image she has of herself as a giving, caring, glamorous goddess of tenderness. And just like you can't change an orange into an apple, or a dog into an airplane, believing that this situation can ever be anything other than what it is, is as futile as trying to play basketball with someone who has no arms – if the armless person was also insisting they were Michael Jordan.

And if, for whatever reason, you agree to one of these arrangements, eventually you will be more disgusted with yourself than anyone else, because you are choosing to live a role in someone else's self-aggrandizing fantasy instead of accepting your limitations, and building something meaningful and genuine and fulfilling of your own.

It's terribly sad, but the worst part about it all is knowing that I will never again play any significant part in Emily's life. I know too much now, and with Mary long gone, Emily is Mom's last best hope to keep a blind follower around.

It is a day of epic humiliations, and horrible revelations that were obvious to almost everyone else in the world who ever cared enough to find out. And since there is nothing I can do about any of it, I spend the remainder of the night feeling pathetic, and crying in Ashley's arms.

14

WEDDING DAY

Now we're in Washington, and this is where the story ends – and the new one begins. The sun is shining, everyone is dressed in their best clothes, and we are in a quaint little town where every home looks like a dollhouse, and every shop looks like it was plucked out of a model train set. I am horribly hung-over, because me and Dylan and Tommy got blazing drunk last night and wound up jamming half a song with the one-man band at the bar where we did most of our damage. I was so smashed, I forgot how to play *Stray Cat Strut* at the lead break, and had to wave the white flag as about a dozen people were hitting the dance floor. After that, I remember stomping around in the woods for some reason, then getting picked up by a lady cop, who let us sing the rest of *Stray Cat Strut* to the guys back at the station over the intercom in her squad car. Then there was spitting. A whole lot of spitting, because my friends pinned me down on the concrete outside of Ashley's childhood home and let me have it until I begged them to stop, which seemed like a fitting, and overtly metaphorical, end to my youth.

But it's not over yet, because I still have to stand in front of all the people assembled here and pledge that I will grow the fuck up already, and try my very hardest to be a responsible young man; and I have to look Ashley in the eye while doing so, and mean it.

And thank heaven for bad news, because there is nothing like it for bringing your priorities into focus.

Ashley had a miscarriage this week, and she is for all intents and purposes still miscarrying at this very moment. And with the insanity that surrounds the planning of a wedding, the buying of engagement and wedding rings on credit, and the traveling of all your friends and relatives to another state - not to mention trying to get to know each other in the middle of an intense dose of familial madness and human molting – losing the baby seemed like the kind of moment when a certain someone might begin to think about running away to join the circus. And I have been, and still was until about a minute ago, when Dylan caught me staring out the window like a condemned man.

"We can leave, you know," he says.

I look up and laugh perhaps the most half-hearted laugh in the history of laughter. We can't leave. A crowd has gathered at the gallows, and they want to see a hangin'. How on earth can we just walk out of here?

"I'm serious," he repeats. "All we have to do is go, and we can do that right now."

Man, that sounds good. All this pressure gone, and I would be free again – free to move back by the college, buy some steroids, and start the whole cycle of my young life over. Free to find another girl and hope for an easier result. Free to end the tension that we can call growing pains, but doesn't hurt any less for the euphemism.

But as I'm having these thoughts, the events of four nights ago sneak up on me. *Bad to the Bone* was playing, and I was behind the bar thanking God that this was the last shift I'd have to work until I got back from Washington. I was waiting for the nonsense to start, when all of the sudden, the girls came for me. Then, as is the custom, I was marched up on the stage, parked in the dirthead chair, and all twenty of the dancers who were working that night surround me with their boobs out, and began planting incriminating kisses all over my face and neck, and particularly on my white shirt.

It was actually pretty fun, but even in that moment I could tell it was a mirage. Like Disneyland is a blast when you're ten, but what if you couldn't leave? How would it feel then? You might eventually miss your home, and when puberty hit, maybe you'd want to be somewhere quiet, with someone you liked, and start figuring out that part of your life. You'd probably hunger for something to do besides riding the rides, and soon you'd see past the façade to the machines working the contraptions, and the employees frowning and smoking when no one was looking. You'd probably get sick to death of cotton candy and hot dogs, and maybe you'd want to see the ocean, and even something that isn't designed to perpetuate a fantasy.

I was grateful that all of these people thought enough of me to care that I was getting married, but, truth be told, I'd already seen all their boobs a million times, so the sparkle was kind off of the situation — and I still hated *Bad to the Bone*.

Then I was back in the hotel with Dylan, thinking about how Ashley saved Emily, and realizing that she wasn't my mother, and I wasn't my father. And because I was about to marry one of the best people I'd ever met, I didn't even have to be me anymore, because here was the golden opportunity I'd been waiting for to quit dicking around already, and get down to business.

"I'm ready for this," I tell Dylan, and the next thing I know Ashley is walking down the aisle toward me, and then the crowd is clapping, music is playing, and we are hitched.

At the reception following the wedding, my whole life flashes before my eyes — because many of the prominent players in it are here. My dad and I get to spend some time together, and there is clearly an opening to start that relationship over. Mary misses the wedding, but Mark is here, and we go to the fort on the outskirts of town and talk about life and the future, and it seems like the opportunity is there to return to the Improv if I want to. Of course, Tommy and Dylan are here, and they are heading back to Seattle tonight to tear it up. And then there is Mom, ever the gypsy, who is moving to Kentucky with Ray in a few months. She is on her best behavior in the beginning, but about an hour into the reception she vanishes with Ashley's recently divorced step dad, sending Ray into a rage. He leaves Emily with me and Ashley, and we watch him from the balcony as he storms around town looking for Mom. When he can't find her, he returns, collects Emily, then leaves in a huff – and this is one of the last times I will ever see him.

And then the party is over, and Ashley and I are sitting on the bed in the massive suite where the wedding occurred, waving good-bye to Dylan and Tommy as they head out for the night. Part of me really, really wants to go with them, but that definitely won't be happening.

It's weird; two different couples stopped me today to offer a word of advice. The gist of both of these talks – which were had with Ashley at my side – was, "Marriage is hard work, there are ups and downs, and you have to work through the rough patches, blah, blah, blah." I felt like saying, "Look, thanks, but we've been living together for like five months now, and I boned tons of chicks before that, so save it for someone with a little less experience." The nerve of some people.

Then the door shuts. Dylan and Tommy are gone, and it's just me and Ashley in a big empty room full of hors d'oeuvre trays, wrapping paper, open boxes, empty bottles, plastic glasses and picnic plates. There is a big wooden floor in front of us, where, I guess, we could dance if we wanted to, but God only knows what happens next. To be honest, I'm beginning to think there was a little more to this party than picking out rings and dresses and stationery. Like maybe when you make vows in public, someone is recording those words in your permanent record. And I'm not about to say this in front of anyone, but I'm also beginning to think that this situation might actually be serious.

PART FIVE

EPILOGUE

(A Quick One, I Promise)

EPILOGUE

Our son was born today. He is the first blood relative I have ever seen, and my God is he beautiful. There is so much more to say, but I don't know how to do that in a way that would make sense to another person. However, when I looked him in the eye for the first time, I felt an overpowering sense of understanding between us, so I made him a promise: "Whatever it takes to be the kind of father that you deserve, I will do. And when I fail, I will get back up, correct my mistakes, and try even harder the next time. And most of all, and no matter what, I will never leave you, because you are my son, and I am your dad, and I love you unconditionally, forever."

And I know one more thing now, too: It's worth it. Whatever comes before this moment, and whatever you have to do because of it after, it's all completely worth it.

As a matter of fact, it's a bargain at any price.

THE END

ACKNOWLEDGEMENTS

My deepest gratitude to Curtis Grippe – who has endured countless talks about the subject matter of this book - for his support and encouragement above and beyond what any human being should expect from another. No one has ever had a better friend.

Thanks also to David Dunton of the Harvey Klinger Agency and my attorney Darren Trattner for all of their efforts on my behalf.

I also wish to thank the following people (and dogs) for their various forms of support during the writing, editing, and publishing of this book: Meggins Moore, Travis Collins, Judith Lonsdale, Lori Walker, Spanky, Art Edwards, Alex Sokoloff, Sherrie Petersen, Eric Kowal, Jill Litwin, Julie Moore, Lao Tzu, Keith Richards, Willie Nelson, my sons, their mom, and the late, great Delilah.

My apologies to anyone who may disagree with my version of events. You may be right. I may be crazy. But we didn't start the fire. And in all seriousness, if I spent any kind of time talking about you in these pages, our time together meant a lot to me, even if it was difficult.

And finally, thank you God, my parents, and rock'n'roll because if not for you I would have been someone else entirely (though that guy may have had more money).

ABOUT THE AUTHOR

CRAIG MACHEN wrote the movie *Wasted* for MTV, and for the Zac Efron show *Summerland*. In 15 years of film and television writing, he has worked for Ben Stiller's Red Hour Films, Ivan Reitman's Montecito Picture Company, Warner Brothers Television, Jim Henson Pictures, The WB, Spelling Television, Fox Animation, Paramount TV, Tollin-Robbins Productions, Viacom, VH-1, 20th Century Fox, DreamWorks and others. This is his first book.

For more information about the author, please visit
www.CraigMachen.com.

Made in the USA
Charleston, SC
07 July 2011